The Path to Resilience

The Path to Resilience

SEVERINE DESROSIERS

This book is a ***memoir****. It reflects the author's present recollections of experiences over time. Some names and characteristics have been changed, some events have been compressed, and some dialogue has been recreated.*

Design Grade Design and Adeline Media, London

First print February 2021

CONTENTS

PROLOGUE

They say, "You never know how strong you are until being strong is the only option left." I didn't know what that meant exactly until later on in life. When I was younger, I always assumed I'd be the type of girl who would live in the same town her entire life; not a world citizen and certainly not an illegal one. My 34-years on this earth so far have been interesting, filled with significant moments along with horrible ones, but ultimately, they have made me the resilient woman I am today.

1

WE ARE FAMILY: DELPHINE, SEVERINE, AND BRIDGET

Delphine was brushing her doll's hair, carefully making sure the bow was perfectly placed in the middle of her head. It was almost time for "Delphine and I's fashion show" we put on in the hallway. I wanted my doll to wear the blue skirt Delphine had put aside, but as I reached for it, Delphine snatched it.

"No! I picked it out first so it's mine," she screamed. I wanted to change her mind, so I put on my best crocodile tears in an attempt to get my way, but she just kept on about her business. I learned to share and wait for my turn that day.

Delphine and I got along some of the time and had our ups and downs like most sisters. She was the golden child; perfect according to Mom and Dad and had taken her role as a big sister / miniature parent, very seriously. This created a barrier between us and the fact that she was more of a loner who liked to keep to herself, leaving me forever yearning for us to be closer. On most of the occasions I tried hanging out with Delphine, she would push me away. Feeling powerless, I promised myself to do better if I ever had a little sister.

On a hot summer day in August of 1991, my younger sister, Bridget, was born. This completed the family with Mom and Dad, Delphine, myself, and now Bridget; all three of us sisters being four and a half years apart thanks to Mom and Dad's meticulous planning. Mom always said she didn't want to have another kid until the previous one could dress themselves and was going to school. There was also our half -sister from Dad, Carlene. Carlene was older than us and lived with Mom and Dad briefly before Bridget and I were born. Mom and Dad rarely ever mentioned her, so I grew up being unsure of who she was and how she fit in the family as it was always just the 5 of us.

Mom was the kind of woman who took pride in appearance. Back in her teenage days, she was amongst the popular kids at her school. She was fair skinned, with naturally long, soft hair, and an angelic face; every boy in school wanted to be around her. Part of me suspects she was born with little heels on her feet because she wore them every single day. It didn't matter if this was to get the mail, or to go on a hike, she had a pair of heels for every occasion. She didn't own a pair of sneakers until she was in her sixties. She always had a complex regarding her height because she was only four foot eleven and felt flat shoes would accentuate this more. When the time came to give birth to Bridget, Mom did so with flawless makeup, not a single hair strand out of place, and after a few days, walked out of the hospital cradling her new baby whilst wearing a pair of tailored shorts, an off the shoulder top, and red wedges.

When Mom's friends and neighbors came to the house to see Bridget for the first time, they were under the impression Mom was getting ready to go to a cocktail party.

For this, I thought Mom and Dad fit well together. Dad was the sort of man who would always strive to be desired and wanted to remain a lady's man for as long as he could. Like Mom, he also took great care of his appearance. Yves Saint Laurent was his signature perfume and at the hospital where he worked, his colleagues could locate him, based on how much of the perfume they could smell in the air.

Despite being married with 4 daughters, Dad led his life like a bachelor. At times I wondered if he was actually ready for kids; that being said, he would always make sure we had everything we needed.

The day Bridget came home from the hospital was the same day I stopped playing with dolls. *"Why bother with plastic things when I have a real live one right here!"* I thought. I had my partner in crime and would strive to be a great big sister; a standard I try and keep to this day.

Bridget was shy, especially around people she did not know; but because she and I were always together, she found it easy to talk to me when she learned to speak and was even a chatterbox. Two days after her first day of school, the teachers advised Mom to take her to a school with other mute kids in order to fit in better. Mom who was flabbergasted, had to convince the teachers Bridget could speak and wouldn't stop talking at home.

As for me, I was outgoing, always eager to make friends and speak to people. I had a lot of energy and was known to break everything in my path. On the occasions Mom needed to find someone to look after me, it would take two babysitters to keep up with me. At school, the teachers thought I was pleasant to be around and yet I would always get into trouble one way or another.

We had pool days every once in while at the school. One day when the teachers were getting the kiddie pools set up, and we were meant to put on our bathing suits, I convinced my friend, Laure, to go rogue with me and go to the park on the other side of the street instead. We had to hurry; the other kids had already started lining up to get in the water. There was no time to put our bathing suits on, so Laure and I ran to the other side of the streets naked. The two of us were having the time of our lives swinging on the swings fully nude. Unfortunately, this only lasted about 2 minutes before the police pulled up. Naturally, the teachers panicked as they'd lost two small naked children and called the cops right away. I got into HUGE trouble that day but looking back at this event, I thank goodness we didn't get kidnapped.

As I got to Elementary school, I started to notice boys. I had a crush on a boy named Remy. He was a short Italian kid with dark hair and piercing green eyes, who's dimples became more enchanting each time he smiled. I liked Remy and showed my affection the way most little kids do; by throwing pebbles or rocks at him. I did this so he would chase me and for those few minutes, I had all his attention. It was not long after chasing me every single day for about a week that Remy got annoyed and ignored me. Angry at the way he was handling the situation, I started throwing bigger pebbles, and when that stopped working, I threw rocks.

I was throwing rocks at Remy during recess one day, and he ignored me. He continued talking with his friends as though he felt nothing. The more he ignored me, the angrier I became until I looked around and there were no more pebbles nor little rocks; only a large one, about the size of my hand, with a smooth surface. Surprised at the weight of it when I picked it up, I hesitated a little. But watching him ignore me completely reinforced my decision to get his attention back on me, so I threw it at him; I didn't actually want it to hit him and yet it did. To my surprise, it knocked him out for a few seconds. I was horrified.

Needless to say, I got in trouble and the rest of my day was spent at the Principal's office. Remy's Mom showed up to our house later that day demanding to see Mom and Dad. Lucky for me, Delphine answered the door because they were at work. She helped me keep this under wraps and even signed whatever paperwork the principle had sent over regarding this issue. I was in the principal's office so often the staff ended up getting me a special chair next to his desk just for me.

Overall, life in France was easy going, I didn't have a notion of money back then but thought we were rich because we lived in a four-bedroom, two-bathroom townhouse and had a car. I had a closet full of clothes and loads of toys to play with.

The top floor of the townhouse had three bedrooms and a bathroom. Bridget and I were meant to sleep in our own rooms but slept in her room together most nights. Mom and Dad had the second floor to themselves with another bedroom, the living room, and a bathroom.

The wiring was cleverly done so that all the top floor wires could be managed on the second floor. We had a TV on our floor which Delphine, Bridget, and I tried to watch past our bedtimes. We would tip toe over to my room, put the volume as low as possible to watch TV, but each time, Dad would simply pull the plug from his floor and none of us dared to venture down the spiral stairs to plug it back.

Mom and Dad would have us spend our summers with our extended family in Canada and Haiti while they would stay in France and spend time together. Mom and Dad had a couple of brothers and sisters that lived in Canada and the rest of the family were spread out in the US and Haiti. Delphine, Bridget and I would spend one to two weeks per house before moving onto the next Aunt or Uncle. It was great fun since all our Aunts and Uncles had at least two children, so there was no shortage of playmates when we would go visit.

Mom had always dreamt of having bilingual children and really wanted us to learn the English language. She bought us these sets of tapes to help us learn English and would play them all the time in hopes that the language would sink in; instead, my sisters and I memorized the songs mindlessly but didn't care to know what the word meant to teach you.

One day at Delphine's parent/teacher conference, the guidance counsellor told Mom and Dad that Delphine should start looking for a job as a cashier and see if she could make a career out of that. She was only 15 years old and the guidance counsellor had already given up on her. Mom was furious and thought there must be another way.

Not long after that conference, Mom and Dad casually came up to me as I was watching TV to make their announcement.

"We're moving!" Mom and Dad said in unison.

"Moving houses?" I asked, puzzled.

"Moving to a whole other country, America." Dad answered.

"But I like it here." I replied. I scrambled past Mom and Dad's legs and rushed to the safety of my room. I would not be the girl that had grown up in the same town her whole life. I would not be like everyone else; I would be different from now on. *Maybe it won't be so bad, besides, I have little choice anyway.* I thought. I sat up in my bed for what felt like hours, trying to make sense of it all.

To me, this announcement was life- changing; I didn't appreciate it right off the bat, I'd be losing all my friends, starting in a new strange place; but as the years have passed, I've learned to embrace it, made new friends, and even looked forward to seeing new places.

Christmas Day arrived. I woke up to the sound of Mom and Dad moving around on the middle floor. I went down to the living room but there was no Christmas tree, no decorations put up, just an empty house and a couple of suitcases.

"Go get cleaned up and dressed, then come downstairs for breakfast," Dad said as he carried a suitcase downstairs. So, I did. While Bridget and Delphine were getting ready, I went back down and found that two of Mom's friends and neighbors, Paulette and Virginie, were at the door.

"What brings you two beautiful ladies this morning?" Dad asked as he planted a gentle kiss on Virginie's hand. They smirked at each other.

"Move!" Paulette said, rolling her eyes and walking in between them.

"Careful, you almost stepped on my shoes," Dad replied.

I greeted them both while on our way to the kitchen where Mom had prepared some hot chocolate for me and coffee for the guests.

"So, you're still going to go through with this," Virginie said before sipping on her coffee. "Yes, there's no turning back now." Mom replied, her eyes sparkling.

"Roseline, have you really thought this through?" Paulette asked as she leaned closer to Mom. "I mean you have three kids, a mortgage, a car; your husband has been in his job for 20-years."

"Don't forget none of you speak a word of English and you could potentially ruin your kid's lives or emotionally scar them," Virginie added.

"Guys, I've thought of the risks already." Mom said as she grabbed her cup of coffee and stood up. "Now did you come here to tell me what all the neighbors, colleagues, and family members already told me? Or are you going to help me get this luggage in the car?"

"Fine, Fine," Paulette replied, putting her hands up. "I won't try and stop you, there is no going back anyway."

Paulette and Virginie stood up and grabbed suitcases. I finished my breakfast and went back upstairs. I made it a point to spend a few seconds in every room, recording every inch, every detail in my memory to make sure I would remember my childhood home forever. In the middle of the night, we got into the car and said goodbye to our old life, whilst stepping into an unknown world with hopes of achieving the American Dream.

2

THE GEORGIA PEACH

We landed in Atlanta, Georgia, where Dad's brother, Oncle Will picked us up.

He took us to his house, which would be our home for a while. Oncle Will had three kids: Willson, who was twelve, Farah, nine, and Melanie, five. We pulled up to a large red brick home in the middle of the night and found Oncle Will's wife, Tante Beatrice, standing in the driveway, eager to greet us.

We barely had time to put our bags down before she insisted on giving us the grand tour, never mind the fact that we were way past our bedtimes.

"I bet you don't have any houses like these in France," Beatrice stated whilst giving Mom a dirty glance. From the outside, the house did not look like much but once inside, it became apparent that it was divided into three sections. The left-hand side being the basement, but was like a smaller two-bedroom home within itself, the central part, where Willson's family stayed, and the right-hand side, was a one-bedroom apartment that Tante Beatrice and Oncle Willson were still building for us.

We went down to the basement. As Tante Beatrice turned on the lights, the horde of crickets jumped to different corners of the room, hiding amongst the long hair of the dark green carpet. "This is where you guys will be staying; there are two bedrooms for you to share until the apartment out back is ready," she said.

She was right, we hadn't seen any houses like this and up until then, I had never seen a cricket aside from the discovery channel.

Delphine and Bridget walked over to the bed, but I couldn't move, my eyes were fixated on the many crickets in the corners. The more I watched them, the quicker my heart pounded.

"Can she understand me? Do the kids even speak Creole?" Tante Beatrice asked Mom.

"No, not really, we don't speak Creole with them, only French." Mom replied.

"They should understand it, Roseline and I speak Creole to each other all the time, so they've heard creole all their lives." Dad added.

Tante Beatrice put her hand on my shoulder and said, "go on, this is your temporary room. Oh, you're shaking, you must be cold, make sure you get under the blankets." I nodded and slowly joined Delphine and Bridget to the couch.

Over the Christmas holidays, Willson, Farah, Melanie, and I got to know each other. Since all of our parents were born in Haiti, we all tried to speak Creole to each other, which was very difficult since we never actually spoke it. Only Delphine had a good handle on the languages since she had heard Creole longer than Bridget and I plus she had taken some English classes back in France; she hadn't learned much, just a few words here and there, but it was already more than the entire family combined.

Before we knew it, the Christmas holiday was over, and the first day of school arrived. I jumped as the alarm rang and searched for the doorknob in the dark. Unsure the time was right, I went to the kitchen window to check it was daytime. Delphine, Bridget, and I got ready in record time and went up the stairs to the main kitchen for breakfast.

"Wow Roseline, your daughters are pretty and so well dressed." Tante Beatrice said as she was making the coffee.

"Oh thanks, I do not like walking around with children that look like hobos, if they are to walk by my side, they must look the part." Mom replied.

Tante nodded and hastily left the room.

"Uncle Will is coming with us to drop you guys off at school as soon as Willson and Farah are ready," Mom told us.

"Where are they?" Dad asked as he rearranged his tie.

"They will be another couple of minutes, Beatrice is making them change outfits for some reason," Oncle Will replied as grabbed the car keys. We dropped Delphine off first at Walton High School, then headed over to East Cobb Elementary and dropped Bridget off in kindergarten and me in the fourth-grade class. When we got to my classroom, I took a few steps forward confidently then stopped to look back at Mom and Dad with a smile, ignoring the knots in my stomach. They waved and left quicker than I expected.

"Class, here is the student I had told you would come join us; Her name is Severine and, I expect you all to give her a warm greeting." The teacher extended her arm towards my seat. Before my bottom even hit the chair, the kids all came up to my desk to say hello. "Here, a few of us got you red apples." One of the students said while handing one to me. I smiled and slowly ate one during class then put the rest in my bookbag.

Farah found Bridget and I at the end of the school day and we all hopped on the school bus, sitting next to Willson.

"Farah, comment ou dit moin pas reme ça?" I asked her while holding the red apple up.

"I don't like red apples," she responded.

"Qui ça?"

"I. Don't like. Red apples. Why? Where did you get these?"

"The kids in my class gave them to me; I hate red apples but did not know how to say that until now." I repeated the sentence a few more times before getting it right and then ran to Mom when we got home to show off what I had learned.

"Oh wow, you're already speaking some English! That's amazing." Mom replied.

As soon as the one-bedroom apartment Uncle Will and Tante Beatrice were building was finished, Dad went back to France to take care of the house. We saw him now and then as he went regularly back and forth between France and Georgia, but it wasn't the same – he had become a frequent guest at the house instead of being part of the family. I liked the fact that it was an extension of the house; meaning we could see Willson, Farah, or Melanie whenever we wanted, but I wasn't a fan of having to sleep in the living room every night with Delphine and Bridget, nor never being able to invite people over because of such embarrassing sleeping arrangements.

There were days when my Mom asked Delphine, Bridget and I to call Dad and ask when he was coming home for good. I didn't see it then, but the move caused a rough patch in their marriage.

3

GETTING SETTLED

Like most classrooms in the States or anywhere else, one wasn't allowed to get up and leave without the teacher's consent. There was a day when I had to go to the bathroom in the middle of class, but I hadn't yet learned how to ask in English. I tried to hold it until our next break, but was afraid I was going to pee myself. My bladder felt like it was going to explode. Every minute passing felt like an hour, and I could no longer hear the teacher. I went for it. I got up and headed for the door, keeping my legs close together, only to see the school security guard right outside. "Where are you going?!" he yelled. I kept walking, thinking he would eventually see I was going to the toilet, but he caught up with me quicker than I expected. Next thing I knew, I was in the principal's office. (It felt like France all over again.) My ESOL teacher asked me why I'd left the classroom like that. I explained it to her, and she translated for the security officer and the principal, who nodded his head towards the bathroom when he saw me shaking in the chair, trying desperately to hold it in. I galloped to the bathroom and almost missed the toilet seat. *Close call! I really need to know how to say, "I have to go to the bathroom."* The kids at school showed me southern hospitality; they were very welcoming and inclusive, but I still felt isolated by the language barrier. Being unable to communicate with the other kids and continually having to use sign language made me frustrated and sad, but out of that came determination; I would conquer the English language if it was the last thing I did! At home, I watched *The Simpsons.* I've always been a massive fan of the TV show and knew every episode by heart – at least I had when they were in French. When I watched *The Simpsons* in English, I did so attentively, paying attention to what they said in English and comparing to what I remembered them saying in French. This gave me the gist of certain words and phrases. With the help of our ESOL teacher, along with powerful will and determination, both Bridget and I were able to speak some English by the end of the school year but still remained in ESOL classes for another year to perfect our English comprehension and speech.

A year and a half had passed, and Mom finally gathered enough money from her job at Boston Market to move us into a real apartment; they even bought a white, 1987 Plymouth. We moved into a ghetto neighborhood, off Austell Road, and stayed in a three-bedroom apartment. Both Mom and Delphine each had their own bedroom, while Bridget and I had to share. I had no problems sharing with Bridget, as this was much better than our previous living situation.

Delphine was getting older and wanted to be more independent, so Mom and Dad got her a used car, but she needed a license for it first. I was 12-years old at the time, so I didn't know this, but since my family and I had come to the country and overstayed, we were now illegal citizens. This meant we couldn't just go to any DMV and get a license. Instead, Mom and Dad had gotten theirs in Florida, where people didn't ask too many questions concerning paperwork. They arranged for Delphine to go to Florida for a week to get her license and shortly after, a job at the Uptons clothing department store followed. She worked for a few hours every day after school. Delphine was already distant with me compared to how close Bridget and I were, but when she came back from Florida, the distance seemed to have gotten worse; Bridget and I were never allowed to go to her room, and she kept telling me I didn't really know her. I was happy she had gotten the job, but this meant that we really didn't see each other much anymore.

With both Mom and Delphine coming home late, it was up to me to collect Bridget from school, which was right across the street from the apartment. Once home, I would then heat whatever Mom had left for us in the fridge for snacks and dinner depending on if we wanted to wait for them.

I didn't tell Mom nor my sisters this, but I was getting bullied at school by a few girls who lived in the same neighborhood; they would call me names and throw rocks at me when I got off the bus and would taunt me all the way to the apartment. Luckily for me, I now knew how to speak English, but knew little about slang or curse words, so half of the time I couldn't understand what they were saying. Their English differed greatly from the one I learned at school and their accents were something that took me months to get used to. I do know that they would get pissed off from the way I spoke, I had learned to speak English from a white teacher who had lived in California and was in a predominantly white school prior to coming to this predominantly black school. The girls that bullied me didn't understand this, they thought I was 'talking white' to show that I was better than them.

4

DEATH CAN HAPPEN TO SOMEONE YOU KNOW

One day, right before Delphine was getting ready for work, I heard her and Mom arguing. Somehow Mom found out about Delphine meeting a guy when she was in Florida. She started questioning Delphine about him, but Delphine was reluctant to answer, and now Mom was losing her patience.

"How old is he?" Mom asked.

"He's 36." Delphine mumbled.

"That's a lie. I know for a fact that this man has a twenty-five-year-old son, who is still too old for you! You're eighteen years old, for God's sake. You have no business dating such old men!" Mom yelled.

I came out of my room to see what all the commotion was about and saw Delphine telling Mom that she was going to be late for work. With tears in her eyes, she grabbed the keys and headed out the door. Mom didn't say anything to me and just went into her room, so I went back to mine.

Nightfall came, and I woke up in the middle of the night

to pee. I opened the door to the bedroom and saw the hallway lights on. Puzzled, I walked to the living room and found Mom sitting on the couch, looking out the window. The lights were off, but the blinds were opened.

"Mom?"

"Your sister hasn't come home yet. Her shift ended an hour ago." She answered, her gaze never shifting from the window. Without saying a word, I sat next to her on the couch, falling in and out of sleep.

"Come, let's call the police," she said as she gently shook me awake.

Although Bridget and I learned to speak English faster than anyone else in the family, Delphine, as the older sister, was always the one to take care of anything administrative. I felt nervous; I wasn't sure if I would be able to translate everything correctly for Mom. I had learned that 911 was for extreme emergencies. Was this an extreme emergency? Maybe Delphine was late – it wasn't like her, but it was still a possibility. I hesitantly dialed the number, and Mom and I waited, our ears pressed up against the handset. After a ring, someone answered.

"911, what's your emergency?"

"Hi, my sister is missing."

"How old is she?"

"Eighteen."

As soon as the number left my lips, the 911 operator's sense of urgency vanished. She told me I had to wait at least seventy-two hours and then file a missing person's report, or at least I thought that's what she said. I hung up, and Mom looked at me, confused.

"Call the number again," she ordered, and so I did. I must have gotten through to the same lady because she told me the same thing again, but in a very stern tone.

I slowly hung up, looked at Mom and said, "They won't help us."

She looked disappointed. "D'accord. Go to bed; get some sleep," she answered.

I slept for what seemed like ten minutes, but the light in the hallway made it difficult, so I got up again to go check on Mom.

"Delphine just transferred all of her money into my account," she said. I thought nothing of it, but Mom looked anxious. I stayed up with her until my eyes grew too heavy.

Day came, but there was still no sign of Delphine. I went to school with a mild stomach-ache, as if I had a presentation due that I had not prepared for.

That evening, Mom stayed on the couch in the dark again. I left her facing the window, staring into nothingness.

"Allez! Get in the car; we are going to go look for your sister."

I opened my eyes, thinking it was morning, instead it was Mom standing over between Bridget's and my bed, holding onto our jackets. Bridget and I put our shoes and jackets on, then got in the car. Mom drove to Delphine's workplace first, only to find an empty parking lot. She then drove to her school, and then to any other place we could think of, but with no luck. Everything was closed, all parking lots were empty, so we came back home. Bridget and I went back to bed while Mom went back to that same spot on the couch, looking out the window.

My stomach-ache grew worse, as did that nervous feeling. The next day, before Mom came back from work, I left Bridget in the house for a couple of minutes while I went upstairs to speak to one of my only friends, Adriana.

Adriana and I had met on the bus on the way to school. On my first day on the bus, I looked to see where I would sit and came across this girl with long black hair and a face full of pimples. She turned from the window to smile at me with her shiny braces; I immediately sat with her, and we had been sitting next to each other ever since. We didn't have many classes together but chatted about random things on the bus ride to and from school every day. English was not her first language either – her family was from Mexico, so we bonded over the fact that we were both immigrants. Adriana lived only one floor above us, and yet we never went to each other's houses after school, so when I went over that day, she knew it was serious. I knocked on the door twice, and a man who seemed like her older brother or uncle came to the door. "Is Adriana here?" I asked.

He walked me to her room without saying a word. I knocked lightly before opening the door. Unfortunately for her, she was in the middle of getting dressed and didn't have time to put on any pants before I shouted out, "Delphine, my older sister, is missing!" The tears came rolling down my cheeks. She looked at me for a moment and just tapped the bed she was sitting on.

I sat next to her and she gave me a hug, then sat in silence while I cried. She patiently waited until I had calmed down, then hugged me again. "Everything is going to be okay. Wherever she is, I'm sure she feels bad, and she will come home soon," she said.

I believed every single word of it. I believed her because I wanted to, because I had to. I wiped my tears and went home.

Mom came home from work, quickly changed her clothes, and told us to get in the car. We were going out to look for Delphine again. We looked for a couple of hours with no luck, not even a trace. When we got back home, Mom started calling family and any friends of Delphine she knew about until night came; when she sat on the couch yet again, waiting. Watching. The next day at school, the teachers saw I looked different. I was exhausted, with a constant stomach-ache. The nervousness had affected my breathing; I started hyperventilating in class and my social studies teacher pulled me to the side after class.

"What's wrong? Are you okay?" she asked.

"My sister is missing; we don't know where she is."

She put her arm around me. "Come with me." She walked

with me to the guidance counsellor's office. "Wait here for a Moment, okay?" She knocked on his door and walked in. They had a few words before she left me in his care. Until then, I had never even known there was a guidance counsellor's office there, let alone seen it. I walked into the small room with dark red carpet, a wooden desk, and three chairs. A tall, white, bald man with glasses got up from his chair and came around to shake my hand.

"Hello, Severine. I'm Mr. Dulsby."

I shook his hand and sat. Instead of sitting across from me, he pulled up the chair next to me, which made me feel more comfortable. We stayed in his office for a couple of hours. I talked to him about the situation with Delphine, then we started talking about anything and everything. My stomach-ache and nervousness went away the more we talked. That day, on the bus back home, Adriana told me about a friend whose sibling had done the same thing and then came back home. She told me again that Delphine would come home soon. Her story and her words made me hopeful. I got off the bus and walked the short way home with a smile on my face. As it was her day off, I came home to find Mom cooking dinner. "Maman! Adriana said that this happened to one of her friends, and she came back after a little while; this means that Delphine will come home soon. I just know it!"

"Okay, I sure hope so," she replied quietly, while continuing to stir the pot; not bothering to turn around.

I lost my train of thought as I noticed a police car and two policemen out the window. I knew it was a ghetto neighborhood but had never actually seen the cops here. People mostly kept to themselves. Curious as to where they were headed, I ran to the window, pulling the blinds to clearly see, but was interrupted by a knock on the door. I jumped from the couch and ran to the door. To my surprise, the same cops I had seen pass by the window were on our doorstep.

"Hi, is your Mom home?"

"Mama!" I shouted.

As they stepped inside, they took off their hats and asked Mom to sit on the couch, while they sat down across from her.

"We found your daughter's body," one of them said. I'm sure they said much more after that, but it was like my hearing turned off. A feeling like an anchor slowly dropping to the sea floor came at the bottom of my stomach. Every breath I took after that was filled with anguish; all I could hear was myself breathing – or struggling to. I turned to Mom, who fell from the couch and onto the floor. The cops and I rushed to her aid and realized how heavy she was. It was as though her legs hadn't received the message it was time to stand up. We tried a few times to stand her up, but it was no use, she had gone limp. Mom stayed down, crying her eyes out. It seemed that when Delphine left for work after arguing with Mom the other day, she went to a CVS

Pharmacy just down the street from us, purchased sleeping pills, and took a large dose of them in her car. She then put the windows up, wrote us a note, and waited to die. She was in the parking lot for three days before someone found her. It was September, but we were experiencing an Indian summer, making the temperatures higher than normal; on some days, they climbed to eighty degrees, so Delphine's body decomposed quickly. Every time we had gone out to look for her, Mom made a right-hand turn out of our neighborhood to start the search – had she just turned left, we most likely would have spotted her car in that parking lot. We could possibly have saved her, but I guess things were meant to happen as they did. I guess we were not meant to find her at all.

In this family, we have had deaths before. Uncles and grandmothers have died, but neither my sisters nor myself had ever met them, or we had met them once when we were infants. Bridget and I had never really been affected by death until that day. I went to Delphine's room and sat on her bed. A chill came over me; I realized death can happen to someone you know.

5

BREAKING THE NEWS

The cops gave me the note that Delphine had left for us. It said that she couldn't deal with it anymore and that she loved us all. I galloped to the phone and called one of Mom's closest friends, Mrs. Bernard, to break the news. Mrs. Bernard was a friend of the familyand a co-worker Mom had. She was a single woman with two boys between Bridget's and my age. She had helped and inspired my Mom many times, and therefore it felt like she was the most appropriate person to call. After getting off the phone with her, I worked my way down through all family members and friends to break the news.

The cops handed me a bag of gifts Delphine had bought Bridget and me; in it was a tape of the group 'TLC' which Delphine knew I loved. There was also a coloring book meant for Bridget, which she immediately took to our room to get started on the coloring, with TLC playing in the background.

On my way to join her, the back of my throat became heavy and my eyes burned as my lips quivered.

"Severine! Can you please call people and let them know immediately?"

"Yes Mom," I answered, taking a big breath on my way to the phone. I went through a list of people, telling them to come over as soon as they could. It was time to call Dad.

"Don't tell him what's happened, just tell him to get here as soon as possible," Mom instructed. With no hesitation, I dialed the number.

"Dad, something's happened."

"What? What's wrong?"

"Please take the first flight to Atlanta. This is an emergency."

"OK... but tell me what's happened." He was getting frustrated.

"Please just get here as soon as possible. I have to go." The cops asked Mom a couple of questions, collected the TLC tape and coloring book, claiming it was evidence, and advised us to be around friends and family before leaving.

That night Mrs. Bernard came to stay with us. Bridget and I fell asleep despite everything that had been going on. Throughout the next couple of nights, I would wake to the sound of Mom's cries, so I would go to her room, sit on the bed and give her very long hugs until Mrs. Bernard told me to go back to sleep. This happened every couple of hours for several days. As I was walking away from a long hug with Mom one night, I overheard Mrs. Bernard tell Mom in Creole,

"Roseline, I know this hurts, and it's going to be hard for a while, however, you still have two girls that need you, so don't you even *think* of letting go."

Dad came two days after we heard the news. We sat him on the couch before breaking the news to him. What happiness he had in him quickly vanished. He put his hands to his face, but Oncle Will reminded him that real men don't cry. Forced to keep it together, he sat there trying to digest the information and attempting to figure out what went wrong. Life felt very unstable, I was in and out of school, meeting various friends and family members and receiving money left and right from everyone that wanted to help however they could. I decided to go back to school for good. I wanted to feel normal; I wanted a constant because it helped me pretend this wasn't happening.

I would try to stay busy at school and try to take part like I used to, but there were moments when I felt I couldn't breathe. During such times, I'd go to the guidance counsellor's office. He reassured me by telling me that what I felt was perfectly normal. He told me it was OK to cry, but it's not like I didn't want to; the tears just wouldn't come. It was as though my feelings were constipated. He also said that holding in my feelings might lead to me losing it and lashing out one day; and that this wouldn't just happen overnight, that it could even happen a few years from now.

The day of the funeral came and we went to church. Instead of it being filled with strangers, it was filled with friends and family. Right after the service, we drove to the burial site. Mom, Dad, Bridget, and I each had to grab a handful of dirt and throw it onto the closed coffin as it was going down into the ground. As I watched it go down, I tried to feel something, at least sadness, but not a single tear dropped. I was just standing there. For many years, all I felt was anger. *"How could she just leave us like this!"* I thought to myself whenever I even felt sad.

It wasn't until the ninth grade, when I did a book report on depression as this was a topic in my health class, that I got to thinking, I might have been able to prevent it had I known more about it and looked out for the signs of depression. My anger had turned to sadness.

There was no time to process my feelings at the time; instead, I spent my time trying to help Mom the best way I could, which I don't regret. Since Delphine died, it had fallen on me to do all the things she used to do – like all the paperwork and admin. It was a pivotal point in my life because my role changed from being the middle child, the one my Mom and Dad would mostly forget about, to being the older sister from now on, where all eyes were on me.

I still dream about Delphine from time to time. In my dreams, I never remember that she's dead; I just know that she has come back from a long trip. I ask no questions about it. I just try to catch up with her and tell her about everything that has been going on since her 'trip'.

A few days before her death, she came home early from work and saw me trying to record the TV series, Charmed. She quickly put her things down, ran over to me, and started tickling me; she then convinced Bridget to do the same. I never got around to recording the episode that day. Instead, all three of us watched it live. I wasn't angry about this, in fact, I was thankful; I was thankful to have two sisters and thought we are kind of like the three Charmed ones. I did not know about the series of events that would later follow, but I look back on this moment and feel like that was a slight chance to say goodbye; a window of opportunity to be happy for what I have before it gets taken away.

My half-sister, Carlene, came to the funeral, and it was the first time Bridget and I had really met her. She would call from time to time, and Mom would quickly say in passing 'that's your sister', but Bridget and I were too young to comprehend what Mom meant by that. To Bridget and I, a sister is someone who grows up with you, like Delphine did with us.

Having her here with us was strange; we were from different backgrounds and had a little less than two decades of an age difference between us. I wanted to ask why she didn't grow up with us, but obviously, bigger things were going on, so I kept it to myself. The first night she stayed with us, Carlene insisted both Bridget and I sleep with her; in her arms. This was one of the strangest nights I've ever had.

Bridget and I were already close, but going through this brought us even closer. In the house, we rarely spoke of Delphine's death, and since it happened, we've never visited her grave. Mom said she didn't want to revisit the past. I agreed with her; besides, there was too much to do and, therefore, no time to grieve.

6

LIFE AFTER DELPHINE

A few weeks after the funeral, we moved near Terrell Mill Road, Georgia. The home dynamic was different; there were just four of us now. Dad was no longer going back and forth from France to the US; he had gotten a job as a school janitor, had the house rented by family friends. He was here to stay.

We moved to a two-bedroom townhouse where Bridget and I shared an enormous room with plenty of space to run around, which is just what we did. In the time we stayed there, we put a couple of holes in the wall due to rough play, and we broke a couple of twin beds. This move meant changing from Marietta Middle School to East Cobb Middle School. Once again, I was leaving behind the few friends I had made. At the new middle school, I didn't want to be the girl whose sister died, so I didn't tell anyone what had happened and why we had moved. I kept it all to myself. I didn't want to talk too much about it at home because I didn't want Mom, Dad, or Bridget to be sad. So, I kept it to myself. I started reading a lot of Chicken Soup for the Soul books, especially the ones about death, to gain insight on how others may have dealt with it.

Going to the new school was hard at first; I had no real friends and was lonely. It's not like I was ever popular at Marietta Middle School, but now and then, a boy would ask me out. I even had a boyfriend for a short while, but over in East Cobb, a predominantly white school, black girls like myself were usually invisible.

Mom and Dad would leave for work together very early each morning. I would walk Bridget around the corner to the bus stop, then I'd have an hour to myself to get ready for school. There were days when I would start getting ready for school after dropping Bridget off, and I would feel angry – not with anyone in particular, just at everything. I would get so angry that I would cry sometimes, and on those days, I would just skip school. It got to a stage where I had a hard time finishing a school week without skipping at least one day. I never got in trouble for it, and to my knowledge, Mom and Dad knew nothing about this. I'm assuming that somewhere in my transcript the reason for the move was mentioned, and the teachers gave me a pass considering the circumstances.

Toward the second, and last, semester of seventh grade, I met Erica and Iman. Iman was the class joker, originally from Iran, who came to the US at a very young age. Compared to the other cliques in school, like the popular kids, the geeks, and the goths, she and I were outsiders and were proud of it. We had most classes together, like PE, social studies, and language arts.

One day, in our PE class, Iman and I were playing badminton, our favorite game. We took the game seriously and always aimed to beat everyone else. As the birdie flew to Iman, she somehow broke the racket on her head while attempting to hit the birdie – which was hilarious! I fell to the floor in tears since I was laughing so hard. She and I laughed throughout the rest of PE. Our next class was history, where Iman and I sat across from each other. I was trying my best to stay composed, but Iman kept repeating the arm gesture that led to her breaking the racket, causing us to burst out in laughter. Unfortunately for me, the teacher wasn't laughing with us, and she kicked me out of class for being a disturbance. I was laughing so hard that I had to crawl out of class while wiping my tears.

Iman's grades slipped, and her parents weren't happy about it. She started putting distance between us and was now hanging out with a different group of friends. I was upset because it felt like I was losing her. Eventually, she addressed the matter with me. I didn't agree, but she and I talked things out, and I had no choice but to accept the new situation. We stayed friends but were nowhere near as close as we were when we first started hanging out.

Erica and I would hang out from time to time during the seventh grade, but this was only when Iman wasn't available. Erica was an American girl who had lived in Georgia all her life. Like Iman and me, she also was an outsider at school but didn't let this stop her from loving life. She was boy crazy and would have a new crush every other week. Her bubbly personality attracted many friends, but she never had a boyfriend because the guys did not see her that way. In fact, the popular kids dubbed her the ugliest girl in school.

During the summer, I would call Erica now that Iman and I were nothing more than acquaintances. We would spend all day and all night on the phone. I was regularly at her house or vice versa. When eighth grade started, Erica and I were officially best friends. We were so close that we were finishing each other's sentences. We would write each other at least three notes per day and even had days when we would accidentally come to school wearing the same outfit.

Summer came and high school was up next. I wanted to be more involved in activities, since I was never really part of anything before, so I tried out for JROTC (a federal program sponsored by the US military) and volleyball. Tante Judith, Tamara and Nadia's Mom, was having marital issues, so she came to live in Georgia. Meanwhile, we had found a larger apartment just around the corner from our current one. This was the very first move we made that didn't involve switching schools; it was almost weird. Tamara would be a freshman with me, and Nadia was a junior. Tamara had skipped a grade in elementary school, so she was one year younger than me but we were in the same grade. During that summer, my waist became even smaller, and my butt was bigger; I was finally considered cute. I was now fifteen years old, had newfound confidence and told myself that I would no longer be invisible; besides, I was on the volleyball team now, so this would help me make even more friends. When school started, I immediately introduced Tamara to my group of friends. She was beautiful, fun to be around, and smart, so it took no time for her to become very popular in school and eventually get her own group of friends – the type of friends even I was not cute enough to obtain. Any time I didn't have volleyball practice after school, I would get off the school bus at the bus stop in Tamara and Nadia's neighborhood and hang out at their house for a couple of hours. Bridget's bus would also stop on Tamara and Nadia's block, so Tamara and I would wait for her bus to come so that both of us could stay at their house until our Mom and Dad got home.

At school, Bridget was a very shy kid. However, this had changed over the years, since Bridget and I are about five years apart. This meant that after fifth grade, we no longer went to the same school; she was finishing Elementary school while I was entering high school. I continued to drop her off at the bus stop every morning and stayed until she got onto the bus, at Mom and Dad's request. There were so many elementary school kids in our neighborhood that there were two school buses that would come – one for kindergartners to third graders and one for fourth and fifth graders. The bus for the younger kids would come about five to ten minutes after the other bus, but Bridget always insisted on waiting for that bus, saying that it had more space. I didn't really see how it would have more space, especially since Bridget was a fifth grader and was bigger than most of the kids at the bus stop.

One day, as I was waiting with Bridget at the stop, I started looking around at the little kid's faces who were eagerly waiting with their parents for the bus. I waved at one little boy, most likely in kindergarten, who was looking in my direction. He gave me an enormous smile and waved back, but then his eyes widened with fear, and he started crying. I looked around, thinking there was a large dog or a bug next to me, but there was only Bridget and me. Shortly after the buses arrived, I hugged Bridget and waited for her to get on the bus. She got on right after the little boy who was crying. I watched the bus drive away and saw Bridget shoving the boy down the aisle to force him to walk faster. It was then that I realized why the little boy was crying earlier. Bridget had become a bully. She wanted to be on the bus with the younger kids to terrorize them. The next morning as Bridget was getting ready for school, I asked, "Bridget, are you bullying those kids at the bus stop?" Bridget casually answered, "Yes, I'm a big kid now, so they have to do what I say."

7
CROSSROADS

During the middle of the year, we moved to Paulding County, and this resulted in yet another school move in the middle of ninth grade. We were moving into luxury apartments in a neighborhood called St Ives. St Ives was nothing short of wonderful; we had a three-bedroom apartment on the seventh floor with a large balcony. My room was rather small, but it was perfect, as there was a lot of light coming in which I loved. Also, within the clubhouse was a gym and a pool that always seemed to have free food available. The only inconvenience was that if you wanted to buy some milk, you'd have to drive 15-20 minutes to the nearest store and then carry this up to the 7th floor since there was no elevator. Since we moved to Georgia, we had lived in Cobb County, but now since we had moved over to Paulding County, we soon learned it was a more 'up and coming' county, and that there was not much to do. We literally had one Walmart, a gas station, and an old movie theatre. At one point, it was one of the fastest-growing counties in America; there was always something new being built.

I stayed in faint contact with Iman, but mainly stayed in touch with Erica and Tamara. Erica would stay over in the new apartment now and then, and we would go to Six Flags in the summer. We still called each other every day, and since three-way calling was here, she would always get us on the line with a boy she knew either from another school or from her childhood. One day she and I were on the phone for a couple of hours and became bored but didn't want to get off the phone, so Erica called one of her childhood friends, Lamar. She introduced us on the phone, and we all began chatting about anything and everything. Lamar was the same age as us, but his voice was so deep that he sounded older and more mature. He and I got on really well, so it didn't take long for him to ask for my number and start calling me without Erica there, so we could get to know each other better.

My first day at Paulding County High School felt like the fourth grade all over again. The only difference was that people had very thick southern accents. Pretty much every single person I ran into was friendly, and eager to help me with anything I needed. In some of my classes, I had kids fighting over me, just so I could sit next to them. Everyone was great to be around, except for a group of black girls. I didn't see it at first because being in a super southern place like Paulding County, all you felt was the southern hospitality, which could sometimes overshadow the occasional racism.

Maybe I would have been oblivious to this if it had happened in the past, but it was my first time experiencing racism; well reverse racism. In Paulding High School, people that came to school early would go to the cafeteria to get breakfast and chat prior to homeroom. I sat in the cafeteria one day, deciding if I were hungry enough to get breakfast when a group of black girls came over to me and tapped me on the shoulder.

"Hi, I'm Tia, and this is Lakeesha, and Lexus, come over! Sit with us."

I was happy to have received an invitation, but that feeling quickly turned to awkwardness the moment I sat in the group. The girls were ghetto and spoke differently than the rest of the people at the school. I could just about make out what it was they were talking about. It didn't take long to realize we had absolutely nothing in common apart from our skin color. I hung out with them a couple more mornings out of sheer politeness until one day; I noticed Jessica also went to this school. Jessica was a friend I had met through Iman back in the eighth grade. She was a big girl with an even bigger personality and was a blast to be around. As soon as I noticed her, I got up from that group, walked up behind Jessica, and tapped her on her shoulder. As she turned around, her big blue eyes widened. She screamed as she tightly wrapped her arms around me.

"Duuuuuude! How the hell are you? What are you doing here?"

"We moved, and now I'm here," I responded.

"Come, come. Meet the gang!" She grabbed my hand and took me to her friends.

Within that circle of friends was a very cute white boy named Chris. He was tall, with an athletic build and piercing hazel eyes. As soon as Jessica introduced me to him, he came closer and looked at me in the eyes.

"Nice to meet you, let me know if you need anything," he spoke, as he extended his hand out for a formal shake.

Mesmerized, all I could do is nod my head and slowly shake his hand. It turns out Chris was mesmerized too. A few notes and a couple of almost inappropriate hugs later, Chris and I were officially an item.

Meanwhile, the group of black girls got pissed that I suddenly stopped hanging out with them, and didn't understand why I wanted to hang around Jessica's group and not them. I was walking down the hall one day when they stopped me by the lockers and made a circle around me.

"Why you always be hanging with these white folks?"

"No wonder you talk white," Lakeesha added as she rolled her eyes.

"I bet you act like it too."

"You think you're too good to hang with us?"

Before I could answer, a teacher came by and told us all to get to class. Afraid that I might get beaten up, I went to the principal's office, who got them to leave me alone.

Chris and I broke up after a month of dating because he wanted to make out with me and got tired of waiting. It's not like I didn't want to make out with him, I would always get nervous then would just end up hugging him instead of kissing him. I had kissed a boy before but didn't have the experience to make the first move or anything, so instead, we remained friends.

8

THE HOUSE AT THE BOTTOM OF THE HILL

On the weekends, Mom, Dad, Bridget, and I would drive around and look at open houses. We'd drive into neighborhoods that had houses selling for millions of dollars and visit just for the sake of it. One weekend, we drove into a neighborhood called Highland Grove; It was picture perfect, with a white picket fence kind of neighborhood (minus the fence) all the houses were placed in a uniform like fashion. As we drove further into the complex, I noticed a big, white house at the bottom of the hill. It stood out from the rest, by somehow being brighter, taller, and wider than the others. I pointed to it and said, "I like that one!" Dad immediately parked the car into the house's driveway, so we could go look.

We opened the door to a bright entrance with rainbow-shaped walls separating the rooms. You could see the back door on the other end of the main hallway, giving you a glimpse of the yard. The living room on the right had the realtor's desk which led to another rainbow shaped- wall, and into a spacious kitchen and a living room. Upstairs had 5 bedrooms and two bathrooms. The master bedroom had an ensuite with a tall cupboard meant to be the men's closet and what looked like a runway for the woman's walk-in closet. We quickly fell in love with the house, and after a few weeks of comparing it with other houses, Mom and Dad announced they had put in an offer. We were moving again! Of course, this meant changing high schools for the third time. By now moving was in my blood; I got used to being in a new environment like a chameleon changes color.

Once again, I was the new girl, but things were different compared to Paulding Co. High. Here there was no one to greet you or help if you were to get lost. On my first day, I was escorted to homeroom by another student. As soon as I walked in, the teacher got up to introduce me. "Class, this is Severine, she is a transfer student from Paulding Co. High." A few students turned to take a glance at me up and down, then quickly got back to what they were doing. *It's going to be hard to make friends.* It took some time and getting used to, but I eventually made new friends. Amongst them was a girl named Kim.

Kim was one of the few girls who came up and introduced herself to me in my science class. We immediately got on. She would invite me as a guest to her church and would stay over at the house or vice versa. When Lamar and I got more friendly and arranged our first meeting at the movies, she helped me set this up by getting her parents to drop us off at the same movie theatre Lamar would be at so we could finally see each other in the flesh. We never saw each other much since Mom and Dad did not allow boys in the house, but he and I always kept in touch on the phone.

9
SUMMER WITH THE COUSINS

A few weeks later, Dad announced we would go to Florida for a few days. It wasn't our first time going to Florida, but Bridget and I couldn't contain our excitement. We went to Kissimmee, Florida, where we got roped in a time-share presentation. One had to stay a minimum of four hours to be treated to a free breakfastand then get free Disney World tickets. We then headed over to Fort Lauderdale to stay with Oncle Evens, one of Mom's younger brothers.

Oncle Evens had three kids; amongst them was Pierre, who was about one year older than me. We stayed at Oncle Evens's house which looked run down with worn brown paint on the outside and few windows to allow for natural light on the inside. We all stayed in one room because Oncle Roland, Mom's older brother, was also staying there with his two kids. We were all just a few years apart, so got along very well and hung out together. As a group with just the kids, we went to the beach, the mall, and spent as much time together as we could during the four days we were there.

On our last day, we all sat in the living room crying because the best four days of our lives were ending. We were mostly sad because the last time we had seen each other was when Mom and Dad used to send us to Canada and Haiti for the summer when we lived in France. Another decade could easily pass by before we would see each other again. On the fifth day, before the break of dawn, we drove back home. Mom and Dad got back to work while Bridget and I got back to our summer routine, babysitting.

Our babysitting gig started because Bridget and I were looking to make some cash. Meanwhile, our family hairdresser, Guerlande, needed someone to watch her kids. Guerlande was about two decades older than us. Back in her day, she was a wild child known for her provocative outfits and gangster boyfriends. Mom always said that the reason she came to Georgia was because her then-boyfriend, who was also a drug dealer, put a hit on her. Unable to go to the police for help because she feared getting arrested, Guerlande's uncle snuck her into the trunk of his car and drove across the state line to Georgia. She settled in Georgia where she had two daughters: Nadia and Cassandra. The two were like little dolls, clever and fun to hang around. Bridget and I would babysit them every Saturday.

One day Mom came home and slammed the door behind her. She aggressively slammed her bag on the kitchen table.

"What's wrong?" I asked, praying she was not crossed with Bridget and I.

"My colleagues at Chick-Fil-A pissed me off. They think because I'm an immigrant, and I don't speak English very well that I have no education!"

"But didn't you finish school in Haiti?" I frowned in confusion.

"Yes but – " she sighed "in these kinds of countries, it's very difficult to get a transcript, especially since I left school a couple of decades ago."

"Well maybe you can just get your GED here then" I replied with a smile.

"What do you mean?"

"There are loads of online schools here, we can just sign you up and you get your GED here; I know you can do this and I'll even help you."

"Okay, okay I'll do it!" she replied.

Shortly after I signed Mom up, we received the first books and exams for her to take and send back to get graded. Mom and I went through this every other day after work or when she could spare a few minutes. We made it all the way to the final exam for her to get her GED. I was pretty good in English and history, but math and science were my weak points. Lucky for me, Oncle Roland and Oncle Evens came to see our new house! I was so excited since we had had such a good time a few weeks back in Florida. I was especially glad to have Pierre come because he was one year older than me and therefore one school year ahead, and he also happened to be a math and science whiz. I told Pierre about the dilemma, and he agreed to take the math and science part of the exam while I took on the English and history part.

We both locked ourselves in one of the guest rooms of the house and took the final exam for Mom. I was about to enter my junior year in high school but still felt confident enough to take the test for her. I knew that between Pierre and I, there was no way we couldn't ace this. We sent the paper in, and a few days later, Mom got her GED certificate in the mail along with a small key-chain version of the certificate. She proudly went back to work waving that keychain in all her colleague's face.

Mom is an ambitious woman and didn't stay satisfied with just the GED for long, so she had me help her sign up to get a certification to become a nurse's assistant. Once again, we got the paperwork for distance learning, and this time Bridget and I took turns reading through the workbooks with Mom. Her English wasn't great, but her determination got her to speak enough English to carry a conversation and comprehend complex reading materials in no time. She could also comprehend most of the material Bridget and I read through and ended up killing it on her final exam! She then worked both at Chick-fil-A as a cashier and the WellStar Hospital as a nurse's assistant.

10
MEETING DIAMOND

Over the summer, I tried to take myself more seriously and would carefully plan my outfits, making sure to look my best at all times. I was dabbling in makeup and got into using Mom's foundation, which gave me the appearance of having a silky-smooth face. I stopped having pimples back in the ninth grade but still used the foundation to enhance my look. By the time junior year started, I was still not popular, but was recognized as somewhat pretty, so people were friendly to me, and boys talked to me, regardless. People thought I was weird and would say I "sound white" yet remained nice to me even though they never attempted to be my friend.

I didn't have many classes with my previous friends, so we strived to meet up in the library in the mornings before school. Among the group was Rachel who was always nice to me and had been keen to become my friend from the moment we met. It surprised me how quickly Rachel became a fan of mine, the kind of girl that compliments you every two minutes, and praises and/or agrees with everything you say. She liked to be seen with me, almost as a way to raise her social status at school. I had invited her to the house once, but when I introduced her to Bridget, Bridget looked puzzled, as though she didn't understand why I was friends with her. As soon as Rachel went to another room, Bridget looked at me and said, "Don't bring her to the house again; she's really ugly." I took Bridget's advice and never bought Rachel back to the house after that.

There was also Kaleiah, who lived nearby and would always sit next to me on the bus. Kaleiah had all the components needed to become the most popular girl in school if she wanted, according to high school standards. She was a shy, God-fearing woman who preferred books rather than popularity which I admired. We made it a point to always meet in the mornings and catch up on life, boys, and everything else.

One day in history class, a new girl came, Diamond Williams. A dark-skinned girl with thick shoulder length hair. Not only was she beautiful, but she was also very smart. She was given the option to skip a grade, but choose not to because she found it important to grow up with kids around her age. Diamond had moved from Washington because her Dad was in the army. Throughout her first days at East Paulding High, everyone whispered about her and would say things like, "Wow, who's that? Who's that girl?"

I introduced myself to her and then introduced her to my group of friends. She was so shy - I honestly wasn't sure if she liked me at all! There would be days when we'd be standing around with the rest of the girls, talking, and Diamond would just walk away without saying goodbye or anything. Since I would see her again the next morning, I figured she was fine hanging out in our group after all. Plus, everyone liked her; well, everyone except for Rachel. Rachel seemed to be jealous of Diamond, possibly because she could see that she and I were quickly becoming close friends. Until this point, Rachel was like Kaleiah's and my sidekick. At one point and time, I suspected she liked me as more than a friend because of how protective she was of me, and she would write me notes that said things like, "I think of you at night, right before going to sleep."

When walking into school one day, I noticed the winter dance posters. "Guys, we need to get organized for the dance this year."

"I know what you mean, Sevie. I've just realized this is less than one week away! Which, by the way, do you want to get ready at my house? Or we ..."

"Let me stop you right there, Diamond!" Rachel exclaimed as she took her thick glasses off to wipe them down. "Kaleiah, Sevie, and I go to every school event together, and that's never gonna change!"

Diamond's eyes grew wider; she was taken back by Rachel's aggressiveness.

"You're more than welcome to come with us; this isn't written in stone," I said while looking at Rachel, puzzled.

We walked together to our homerooms, but before Rachel could go into her classroom, I pulled on her thick sweater sleeve to stop her. "Um, you wanna tell me what the hell that was all about?"

"What? We always go to events together; I don't see why *she* needs to get involved."

"She's new and trying to make friends; lay off her!"

My words fell on deaf ears. As the weeks went by, Rachel would continue to make passive-aggressive comments and made sure Diamond felt left out.

The boiling point came one day while we were in the cafeteria. Kaleiah, Rachel, Diamond, and I were getting our lunches before picking out a table where we could all fit together. As we went to sit, Diamond sat down, then quickly stood back up to right sit across me instead; a spot that up until now was Rachel's.

Rachel threw her arms up and rolled her eyes. "You're not even supposed to be at this table! Why don't you go sit somewhere else?"

Slamming her lunch on the table, Diamond answered, "What's your problem with me and Sevie? You're like obsessed with her! Are you afraid I'll take her away from you or something?"

"Oh, I just meant that..."

"No, you've had an issue with me since day one! There's Sevie; go pee on her to mark your property!" she slammed her purse on the table. "I'm tired of your crap this end today!"

The entire cafeteria was quiet; all eyes were on us, specifically on Diamond. Up until now, we knew Diamond as this very shy and sweet girl, so this outburst especially shocked people.

"But uh," Rachel sighed as she slowly sat down, pulling her oversized sweater hoodie up over her head. Her scattered hair sticking to her face while her tears salted her tater tots. She quietly ate her lunch while sniffling in between bites.

"So, these tater tots are superb today," I said, trying to change the subject. Diamond, who was reapplying her lipstick, looked over and smiled.

We awkwardly continued our lunch. That day, Diamond made a stand for herself, letting everyone know she is not a pushover and I respected her for it. Rachel stopped meeting up with us in the mornings and grew distant; and Kaleiah eventually ended up being home-schooled. Since she lived down the street from me, I tried to visit her from time to time, but her parents always claimed she wasn't home. And just like that, our little group was dis-banded.

Diamond and I got along well. We hung out as much as we could at school, would do things together on the weekends, and talk all day and all night on the phone. It took no time at all for us to become best friends.

In the summer, we figured out that she was only a five-minute drive away from me, so we spent the entire summer together.

Her Dad bought her a car, and Dad let me use the car from time to time, but only for quick trips. That summer, I got to meet Diamond's family. Diamond was the oldest, with a younger sister, Porsche, and an even younger brother, Floyd. Porsche was five months older than Bridget, and they were in the same class. As soon as I introduced them, they became great friends. Porsche was just as beautiful as Diamond, though compared to Diamond she was fair skinned, even fairer than Bridget's skin tone. She had light brown hair that was down to her shoulders and a beautiful smile. She was very popular at school and known to be hilarious.

Diamond, Porsche, Bridget, and I became this inseparable foursome that would spend all of our days together.

Bridget, thirteen at the time, was very attached to me and still very shy. She would still ask me to pay for things for her since she was too scared to face the cashiers on her own. When it was just the four of us, though, Bridget became a whole new person; Big Bertha was the nickname Porsche gave her. Big Bertha was the polar opposite of Bridget; she was outgoing, strong willed, and not afraid to speak her mind. Big Bertha would confidently pay for things on her own, looking at the cashier in the eye while doing it. Porsche and Bridget's liveliness fed off of each other, and they never ceased making Diamond and I cry tears of laughter. We had inside jokes for days. It didn't take much to go into a laughing frenzy. We would just sit around the house, sometimes playing Uno, but would end up laughing so hard our throats were sore and whatever makeup Diamond and I had on would be completely gone due to tears. We would go out shopping at the mall or spend afternoons in Barnes & Noble, reading about our zodiac signs and our personality traits, or we would just go to the pool. We all had other friends but had become our own little family.

11
SENIOR YEAR

Although we were both in the FBLA (Future Business Leaders of America) Club, Diamond and I had no classes together during our senior year, making it vital to keep up the tradition of meeting at the library every morning.

We had a new student, a boy named James, who had just moved over from Barbados and didn't know anyone at the school. When he walked into homeroom and I heard him speak, I was smitten with his accent and volunteered to introduce him around. I wanted to make sure I was the very first one to date the new Caribbean boy and exchanged numbers with him during our tour of the school.

For the first couple of weeks, everything was fine. Then he started asking about coming over, and because of how strict Mom and Dad were, I didn't dare ask them. He and I would make out from time to time, but he always wanted more, which I didn't feel ready for. His behavior towards me changed when he saw that it just would not happen. He slowly stopped walking me to class and it became harder to get hold of him after school. He began spending time with another girl in his home economics class. She was a junior who befriended James a few weeks after he and I started dating. One day he made a joke about how sparks were flying between them while we were on the phone, and I broke things off.

The breakup was inevitable, but he was mad that I got to it before he did, so he started a rumor saying he'd broken up with me because he found out I was sleeping around. I didn't even react to it, because it was common knowledge that I was still a virgin. People at the school knew my name and who I was, but I wasn't popular enough that this mattered.

Prom became a hot topic in school, prompting everyone to buy tickets and prowl for a date. Diamond was going out with a boy named Patrick, so naturally he would be her prom date. Patrick was tall, dark, and handsome with broad shoulders and a Colgate smile – an all-American, brown-skinned boy. Although popular by default due to being on the football team, Patrick was shy, with little to no life experience under his belt. Unlike most football players, he was still a virgin when he met Diamond.

Since the breakup with James, I was still single. Lamar and I kept in close contact, and we talked about him taking me to my prom, but after doing some calculations, we realized that it just wasn't possible, especially because he was attending college in Virginia. I kept some faint hope that somehow he would find the time and money to make it, but also kept an eye out for another suitor to take me. One day, Bridget and I went with Dad to visit Oncle Will. Gregory, a family friend, also stopped by to visit that day. Gregory was a twenty-two-year-old college graduate who looked like the brown-skinned, life-size version of a Ken doll. As soon as we were introduced, we got on and started flirting. I wasted no time telling Gregory of my dilemma, and he offered to take me to the prom. We exchanged numbers, and before I knew it, we were on the phone every other night when I wasn't on the phone with Lamar. He came over to meet Mom and Dad, which was allowed only because he was a family friend and he was taking me to prom.

A few people had told me what James was saying about me, but I was too infatuated with Gregory to care. Mom and I went shopping one day and found a beautiful sky-blue dress. It had a halter top, mermaid skirt, and a little train in the back, which highlighted my hourglass shape and made me look like a Princess.

Gregory wore a black tuxedo. Diamond, Patrick, Gregory, and I all pitched in to rent a limousine that came to pick us up one house at a time and took us to the venue, where the theme was a red-carpet affair. We walked onto the red carpet and into a beautiful room with lights strung everywhere and a large dancefloor. As I walked towards the door, my eyes met with James, who was inside, standing against the wall and grinned when he saw I was on my own. Little did he know, Gregory was talking to the limo driver and eventually caught up with me, holding my hand so we could walk inside. The highlight of my prom was seeing James's face when he saw Gregory next to me as we walked onto the red carpet and into a spacious room filled with light garland. There were a few tables and chairs around the venue, which we didn't use, as we danced the whole time or walked around talking to different people. After a few hours, we left and got something to eat in Atlanta before parting ways. It was a perfect day.

Gregory and I began dating, but it all felt very public, since Tante Beatrice, Will, Willson, Farah, Mom, and Dad knew about it. Like most, our relationship didn't survive college. He and I kept in faint contact, as he was close to Willson and Farah, but it was nothing like before.

Mom, Dad, Bridget, and I visited a couple of universities that had invited me. They were large, with various buildings so spread out, we had to drive from one part of the campus to the other. A visit to a single university campus could take up to half a day. I also applied to a couple of colleges that invited me to visit.

Compared to the universities, these college campuses were tiny, with few classrooms, usually all in one building. Our college campus visits took only an hour; these were the establishments that advertised several times a day via daytime commercials. Worried about costs, Dad took the liberty of learning just enough English to understand what we were in for financially. During the tours, Mom, Dad, and Bridget happily collected the free swag being given out – sweaters, hats, umbrellas and anything else they were giving away – and just before the end, Dad would raise his hand and ask, "Tuition?" As soon as they stated the price, he would shake his head no, making it the last time we would set foot on that campus again.

After having re-taken my SATs, written my 800-word essay, and done a phone interview, I was accepted into the University of West Mississippi. I applied to an out-of- state school only because I wanted to get the full college experience without Mom and Dad breathing down my neck, and the nine-hour drive to get to UWM was perfect. Diamond got the HOPE Scholarship and attended Kennesaw State University, a thirty-minute drive from her house. Before school started, Diamond, Bridget, Porsche, and I spent as much time as possible together. We went off to the pool a lot more, watched Lifetime movies while commenting and laughing together, spent entire afternoons at Barnes and Noble, making the most of the summer before heading off to the new chapter in our lives.

12

ORIENTATION

Mom, Dad, Bridget, and I drove the nine hours to UWM, where we stayed in a crappy little motel off campus for orientation weekend. Orientation ensures that freshmen meet the professors, know how to get to their classes, and get a taste of campus life. Most of the UWM freshman class grew up together or at least knew one another from high school, making me the odd man out; I was amongst the few out-of-state students and the handful of non-Americans.

The orientation organizers took us around the campus to different classes and showed us the leisure area known as the Dub, a vast space consisting of two floors. The top floor had a huge, empty room dedicated for events. On the right was the library and bookshop with UWM or Greek house swag and all of the books necessary for classes. Downstairs had a ping pong table, top of the line treadmills, and a swimming pool.

We eventually came to the dorm rooms.

"Wow! What a tremendous difference between rooms

– some of them look great while others are like jail cells," I joked to Bridget.

"Yeah, you better hope you have one of the good ones," she responded.

"I know, right?"

My laughter soon shifted to worry as it suddenly hit me. I didn't remember filling out an application for housing. I didn't remember because I never did so!

"Tell Mom and Dad I'll be right back," I whispered to her to avoid drawing attention to myself.

I frantically ran to the next available orientation leader, who pointed to a queue. The shortness of the line had me worried and unsure I would be allocated a dorm on such short notice. My turn came, and I gave the orientation lady sitting on the other side of the table my ID. She put on her glasses and looked at her clipboard for what felt like an hour. Scared of the outcome, I stopped breathing, hoping this could somehow brace me for the bad news.

"You're in luck! We've got two more spots left, and you've got one of them," she stated as she looked up at me and grinned.

I exhaled. She looked down again at her clipboard and seemed confused. 'The only thing is, you won't be in the girl's dorm, and you won't be in the mixed dorm either."

"Oh, so where will I go?" I held my breath again. "You'll be in the boys' dorm," she replied, pointing to the building on my left.

I took a big gulp as my eyes widened.

"Don't worry. The building has been divided. You and the other two girls get the bottom floor to yourselves. The boys will only access the second floor on up with their passes."

"Oh, okay, thanks." Relieved, I went back to the tour with Mom, Dad, and Bridget.

That night was the orientation party, which Bridget and I had been looking forward to since we arrived. I wore black loose pants with a low-cut red top while Bridget wore jeans and a white T-shirt. We didn't want to dress in anything too sexy, otherwise we would have to deal with Mom and Dad.

Bridget and I met up with a couple of girls I befriended during the tour and headed straight to the Dub. In no time at all, my sister and I became the center of attention; people formed a circle around us while we shook our booties to the music. The boys were hitting on us left, right, and center. I always looked younger than Bridget, so college juniors and seniors would hit on her, while fifteen- and sixteen-year-olds would come speak to me. I had to become the uncool older sister and tell the juniors and seniors that she was jailbait. As soon as they heard Bridget's age, they bounded away like deer in the forest.

We drove back to UWM the Sunday before the first day of school, navigating the campus confidently thanks to orientation. As Mom, Dad, Bridget, and I started the back-and-forth trips from the car to the dorm room, I kept looking towards the girl's dorm on the right-hand side, hoping I would see the girls I had met at orientation.

"Excuse you!"

I looked behind me and immediately moved to the side, saving my feet from being rolled over by a buggy. Pushing this buggy was a tall, fair-skinned, thin girl with a dark, shoulder-length bob. She was wearing blue Daisy Dukes and a crop top.

"Sorry, these buggies are hard to manage." She wrestled to turn it away from my feet and towards the building doors.

"I'm Tiana, by the way; my friends call me Ti-Ti." She smiled and extended her hand.

"I'm Sevie," I replied, shaking her hand.

She's really pretty; I wonder if we will be friends, I thought to myself. I noticed she was putting her things in the room, right next to mine. We were unpacking the boxes in my room when Mom came over and handed me a different- looking box. I opened it and looked inside – it held a brand-new blanket, new pillows, socks, medicine, and other little bits and bobs. As I continued to look in the box, I saw Dad bringing in a mini fridge.

"When did you guys buy this?" I asked.

"We thought you would need it. It's just better for you to have it," Mom answered.

"Thanks, guys!" I hugged them both. We stayed in the room and arranged all of my belongings for a couple more hours.

"It's getting late, so we better head home," Dad announced. With every step I took towards the car, it dawned on me – I would soon be left on my own. Excitement and fear were coming over me; this immediately turned to sadness when we stopped in front of the car. I hugged Dad first, then Mom a little longer, and then Bridget the longest. The under-estimation of how much I would miss her made my heart sink. I pulled away, noticing her struggling to hold the tears back. I looked at them one last time while saying goodbye, trying my best to crack a smile. Before she got into the car, Bridget looked back at me, her eyes saying she was going to miss me. The only thing left to do was wave as the car drove out of the parking lot.

I walked back to my room. What once looked like a tiny jail cell of a dorm room became a large, isolating space now that everyone was gone. It was a sunny Sunday, yet all I wanted to do was crawl into the sheets and sob. My head hit the pillow and tears came rolling down when suddenly, I heard a knock on my door. Scrambling to fix the bed and wipe my tears, I opened the door to a short, dark-skinned boy with a muscular body. He looked surprised that I'd even opened the door.

"Hey, um, I noticed you earlier." He smiled but quickly looked away when my eyes met his. "So listen, a couple of people are going to watch a movie in my room – do you want to come?"

"Uh, yeah. Yeah, why not?" I replied, trying to sound like someone who had not just been crying.

"Cool!" he answered, relieved. "I'm Blue. What's your name?"

"I'm Sevie."

"Okay. Grab your stuff if you need. I'll wait right outside." He flashed an enormous smile. I grabbed my pass and phone. *I think college is going to be okay after all.*

13

COLLEGE LIFE

During Orientation, I got paired up with a senior named Kyle who made sure I followed my schedule for the first few weeks. He would drive me to and from my classes while making sure I had something to eat in between. I suspected he had a thing for me because of the way he looked at me from time to time, but I thought of Kyle as my big brother, looking out for his little sister. As the weeks passed by, he and I grew distant; I started getting the hang of college life, but he still checked up on me from time to time and advised me wherever he could.

When I came home on the weekends, Diamond organized small parties for me. Sometimes, just me, Bridget, Diamond, Porsche, and Ivena was more than enough for me; as far as I was concerned, my best friends attended. There were a couple of nights where Diamond and I would go to her college parties. Mom would buy me new clothes and lay them out on my bed for me to find. She would do my hair and pamper me – the weekends home were all about me and I loved it.

During the school week, I tried to keep the tradition of watching our favorite TV shows like Gossip girl or Smallville with Bridget but college life took its toll on me, plus it was hard for me to keep up with my new friends and still call her every night. She eventually got used to watching TV shows on her own, going to the cashier to pay for things on her own, and as she got older, she started seeing how hectic high school life can be and wasn't able to call as much either. I missed how attached to me she used to be and yet was proud to see this strong independent woman she was becoming.

It was strange, I had only attended East Paulding High School, for two years and lived in Paulding County for 4 years, but I was used to seeing the same faces and the same crowds; this gave me a certain level of comfort I didn't know I had until UWM. New territory meant starting from scratch and although I made new friends here and there, it wasn't enough because I wanted most people to know me, just like in high school.

The search for quick popularity didn't last long, I came across a flyer one day, advertising a pageant hosted by the Alpha Phi Alpha fraternity. The prize was the miss Black & Gold title, a representation of what the female version of their Fraternity would look like. Among the categories was talent, evening and casual wear, and a question. I went shopping for my gown and was going to use my linguistic skills for the talent part. A friend gave me a poem to recite about God which I translated into French and made it rhyme in both languages; people thought it was phenomenal and it got me 2nd place which no freshman had ever won before.

Wanting to strike while the iron was hot, I entered a couple of more pageants. A lot of them involved a bikini category, which caught boys' attention; this wasn't a primary goal but was welcomed, as I wanted to meet people and for people to know me.

People all over the campus talked and asked about me. The fact that I was black and not from Africa sparked an interest plus, I could speak French and had small cat- like eyes, so they were fascinated. Some thought of me as 'blackinese,' because of how slanted my eyes were, while others compared my body shape to a Coca-Cola bottle.

My circle of friends grew overnight and thanks to doing pageants back to back, the buzz about me, extended off the campus and onto the high school across the street where people talked about me to their younger siblings. I became spoiled for choice of whom to sit with at lunch and I always had a small crowd of people around me.

Amongst my group of friends, was a girl named Slim. I met her in my marketing class. Slim was a brown skin, angel-faced girl who was 5'8. I had seen her from afar on campus and admired her style, her outfits were like a work of art, meticulously put together and a reflection of her bubbly personality and I appreciated it; especially because

I did the same, so I made it a point to be friends with her. Slim was intriguing, she always looked polished and yet her mannerisms showed that of a girl who grew up in a rough neighborhood. She scared me a little but had a sweet and protective side of her too. One day, we were watching a movie in her dorm room and a sex scene came on, which got very graphic. I got uncomfortable and remembered I had to study for an exam the next day so left her room to go to mine. "I've got to go," I said while getting my purse and making my way out of her room. I barely made two steps outside, when my phone vibrated.

"Hello?"

"Hey girl, why did you leave the room?" she asked.

"Oh, I just have something to do."

"Look if you wanted to masturbate, it's fine, I would look away don't worry,"

"Goodness no!" I said, laughing nervously

"No need to be shy I understand," She responded.

Up until now, I honestly thought she was joking, but realized she was dead serious

"Um ok, not this time, but thanks for the offer." I hung up and laughed to myself *what the hell was that?!?*

This didn't hurt our friendship one bit, I simply never mentioned it again. Slim and I would hop in her car on weekends, drive to her house in Mississippi to collect a few of her stuff or do the laundry then drive back while singing at the top of our lungs to the music on the radio. We hung out so much, we eventually became roommates.

I was becoming comfortable coming up to people and striking up a conversation. In my environmental science class, I noticed a girl who kept to herself and didn't talk to anyone so when the time came to find a partner for a small project, I took the opportunity to introduce myself.

"Hey, wanna be partners?"

"Sure," she answered.

"I'm Sevie,"

"Oh! Sevie? I've heard about you!"

"Really?" Taken back by her response, I asked, "Good things I hope?"

"Yeah, guys talk about you all the time, and say you're really pretty."

"Oh wow, OK."

"Now that I've met you, I can confirm, you really are super cute."

"Thanks!" I grinned. It's funny how these things go, if you hear such compliments from a guy you don't like, it's meaningless; if you hear the same compliment from a guy you like, it makes your day; but to hear this from a pretty girl means the world. Maybe because we understand there are no ulterior motives like trying to get into your panties. When a compliment like this comes from a girl, it's usually genuine.

With my recent growth of friends, the weekends on campus were never quiet. There was always something to do: meet up with friends, go to different parties, play video games in someone's room, or something crazy like studying.

14

PROM ALL OVER AGAIN

On my way back to the gym one Saturday, I heard my name being shouted.

"Sevie! Seeeeeeevvvvvviiiiie!"

I looked around, puzzled.

"Up here! Sevie com'ere!"

I looked up to find Anita shouting and waving to come from her 3rd floor dorm room window. I met Anita at my first pageant. She was one of the pageant volunteers; They helped the contestants get ready by carrying our different outfits, help with hair and makeup, and anything else we needed help with. I'd get super nervous, but Anita had an aura about her that made you calm down. She was this big, dark-skinned girl who dressed like she could be someone's Mom and was sweet. Our friendship developed over the pageants. She made sure she was always my pageant helper and I loved her for it.

I made my way to her room. Before I could even knock, she opened the door, took my hand, and pulled me into the room.

"Sevie, I need your help!" she exclaimed.

"What's up?"

"It's my stepbrother, he doesn't have a prom date."

"What do you mean?"

"His girlfriend dumped him just now and his prom is today! He can't go in there alone. Will you help me?"

"Ugh yeah, what do you want me to do though?"

"Well for starters, I know you have gowns here from the pageants, Sev, can you be his prom date for tonight? It'll make his girlfriend jealous, and he can have a good time. What do you say?"

"Yeah sure," I shrugged "I wasn't doing anything in particular tonight anyway; let's do it."

"Oh, that's great because I already told him we were on our way."

"What?!?"

"There's no time Sev, hurry and shower!" She grabbed my room key out of my hand.

"While you do that, I'll go get your clothes. Here's a clean towel," she said as she threw it at me. "Now GO GO GO!" she shouts as the puts both hands on my shoulder and guides me to the shower

I quickly showered as quickly and came back to her room which now had Anita and two other girls who were steam pressing my high school prom dress and laying some makeup on the table. I barely had time to put my clothes on before they started powdering my face. Anita and her friends got me ready and dolled up in about 20 minutes. She grabbed my hand and took me to the elevator. We jumped in her car and rushed to her stepbrother's house.

"We might make it on time," she said. I looked at her and smiled.

"You don't mind, do you?" she asked apologetically. "No, not at all, I'm happy to do it even," I replied, trying to reassure her.

"Thanks Sevie, I appreciate it. I owe you one."

"No you don't Anita. And you're very welcome,"

We made it to her house. I was getting my dress together to step out of her truck when my door opens. A tall, far skinned, charming boy with piercing hazel eyes extends his hand out to me.

"Here, let me help you with that," he said.

"Thanks." I grabbed his hand and jumped out of the truck.

"Hi, I'm Kalvin, I'll be taking you to my prom tonight if that's all right with you?"

"I'm Sevie."

"I know who you are." He smiled as he kissed my hand.

"So, Sevie, are you okay to go with me? You'd be doing me a huge favor" he asked as he looked straight into my eyes. He was charming. It made me wonder why his girlfriend dumped him.

"Let's do it! Where's your car?"

I gave Anita a hug goodbye and walked with him to his car.

We arrived at his prom, which took place in an embellished gym. I felt the eyes staring at me, maybe because I am a stranger to them. This reminded me of prom with Gregory and people were staring at him. Kalvin spotted his group of friends, so we joined them.

"Daaaaaaaaamn Kalvin that's yours?" One guy said while pointing at me. Kalvin grabs me by the waist closer to him.

"Yeah, she's mine," he answered while looking at me.

"You don't mind, do you?" he whispered in my ear.

"We're good, I'll tell you if I have an issue," I whispered back.

We mostly stayed amongst his group of friends, only breaking off to dance now and then. I never saw his girlfriend, nor did his friends even mention her. The prom was coming to a natural end, so Kalvin drove me back to campus.

"Thanks again for coming with me, you're a lifesaver."

"My pleasure, something similar happened to me when I was a senior, so I understand what it's like."

"Oh really? Well, did you have an enjoyable time tonight?"

"I did thanks."

He leaned over to kiss me, but I purposely gave him a kiss on the cheek instead.

"Goodnight Kalvin."

"Goodnight," he responded and smiled. He helped me out of the car and gave me a hug. I walked back to my dorm room. *What a day!*

15

THE VIDEO

Facebook was a year old and having an address ending with '.edu' was a requirement to sign up. I created my account which quickly came with a flood of friend requests and I accepted them all. I wanted to have as many friends as possible. It didn't take long for boys to message me, asking to come over my dorm or for me to come over. Most of these guys had girlfriends, so would only message on the weekends and thought I was too stupid to look at their profile that stated "In a relationship".

I was playing video games with a couple of friends one day, when they asked me about relationships and guys altogether, so I mentioned Lamar.

"Lamar Smart?" One of them asked. I turned to see a dark brown skin, 6'4, heavy guy with dreads.

"Yeah, why do you know him?" I asked.

"Know him? I grew up with the guy!"

"You're kidding?" I asked, fully turning to face him.

"He used to come over to my house so my Mom could baby-sit him while his Mom was out teaching. Me and my brother would always get in trouble and get whippings while Lamar just sat back, eating chips, minding his own business," he explained.

"Cool, small world isn't it?" I smiled.

"Call him, let me speak to him, tell him you're him with Kshun."

I dialed the number and handed it straight to Kshun who spoke with him for 10minutes before hanging up.

"He asked that I look after you," Kshun announced while handing me my phone back.

"Okay, what is that supposed to mean?"

"Just let me know if you need anything okay?"

I nodded yes and watched him leave the room. Kshun and I started hanging out more after that; we would play video games or watch movies with friends. I even convinced Mom and Dad to let him take me home and back to campus from time to time since he was among the handful of people that lived in Georgia. He would go around letting everyone know I was Lamar's girlfriend and say things like 'she's weird as hell bro' while winking at me as his own way to say he doesn't mean it. He called me over to his room one day and seemed excited to show me something. When I walked in, he grinned.

"Here, watch this," he said as he handed me a camcorder. I had never seen him so giddy before so without a word I sat and watched as he stepped out of the room. The video showed Kshun with his friends celebrating his birthday party when a girl entered their room. She danced around for a few minutes, then started removing her clothes one article at a time while the boys started touching her. She then slept with K-shun while his friends were cheering him on. She looked straight into the camera and smiled. My jaw dropped as I froze, leaning into the screen, I exclaimed "Oh my gosh!"

"What?" Kshun asked as he walked back into the room.

"I know that girl! It's Clara!"

"Yeah, so?" He scuffs

"I've got to go." I left the room, furious. *How could he do this to her! Share the video like that! What a jerk!*

Later that day, I saw her on my way to the cafeteria.

"Hey Clara, wait up."

"Hey what's up?" She turned and smiled.

"Hey" I put one hand on her shoulder and looked at her with sympathy "Are you okay?"

"Yeah girl, yeah I'm fine, how are you?" She looked at me like I had two heads for even asking this way.

"I'm okay. So I—"

"Oh, wait a minute, I want to give you something." She reaches into her purse and hands me a CD.

"What's that?"

"It's a video of me sleeping with this guy for his birthday," she answers casually.

At a loss for words, I just stood there looking confused with the CD in my hand.

"Make sure you give it to all your friends, and let them know who I am, I want to get my name out there, I want to be a star!"

"Okay."

"I've got a go, but I'll see you around."

Stunned, I put the CD away. Here I was thinking, this poor girl was humiliated by being filmed on camera while sleeping with K-Shun with his friends in the room, but had no idea she orchestrated it and she wanted it to be out there. *You know what, to each their own if this is how she wants to make her fame, who am I to judge?*

16

THE LAUNDRY ROOM

I was thoroughly enjoying being a college student but especially the newfound freedom that came with it. Mom and Dad had barely let me go out to the movies past 8:00 p.m. back home, yet here I start getting ready to go to the club with either Slim or TT at 9:00p.m. or 10:00 p.m. every weekend. Anyone who looked at me for more than five minutes could tell I was a sheltered kid, but I wasn't the only one. Sheltered kids stick out like sore thumbs – at parties, you can usually find us on top of a table somewhere, in a drinking contest, or first in line to try drugs. I always thought keeping kids sheltered was like failing to open a can of soda that has been shaken; by the time you open it, the soda bursts out, and we sheltered kids are no different. We desperately want to experience everything we ever missed out on, all in one night, as if the world were going to end in the morning.

TT and I were dropped off at our dorm after partying at the Oak Tree one night. We were so drunk we had to hold each other to walk. We did so with baby steps yet somehow still fell flat on our faces right outside our building. We stumbled into her room and I crashed on it.

"Oh, girl, sorry – you can't stay," she stated.

"Aw, is Tony coming over?" I asked, disappointed.

"No, I'm gonna sneak upstairs to see him."

"Dude, you can barely stand right now, and the left side of your face is still red from the fall."

She kissed her teeth and wobbled towards the door. "Girl, this is stupid; just go so I can hurry up and see my boo."

"Whatever." I walked to my room and was out for the night.

The sound of people laughing right outside my window woke me the next morning. I went to TT's door and knocked for a few minutes while trying not to throw up. She opened the door and looked at me for a minute, her eyes red and her face even puffier than last night. She had been crying.

"What's—"

"They took advantage of me!" She wrapped her arms around me as she started sobbing uncontrollably.

"TT, what happened to you?" I asked as I sat her down on the bed.

She was trying to gather herself. "Um, so, I think... I think they all had sex with me. I can't really remember what happened after I went up to see Tony, but I woke up in the laundry room."

"What?!"

She grabbed her bag and continued to wipe her tears.

"Girl, I gotta go. I have to get to class. Don't tell anyone, okay?"

I left just as quickly as I came in and was horrified. I got ready and went to class. On my way, I heard people talking about TT, saying she had sex with the entire basketball team in the laundry room. I didn't want to get too involved or talk about it since I didn't really know what went on. In class, that was all people were whispering about; the rumor was spreading like wildfire in a matter of a few hours. I waited for TT to come back to her room, but she never did.

The next day she asked me to come with her and speak with the dean. I had never actually seen the dean before. I had only received a general "Welcome to UWM" letter with his picture at the top but hadn't seen him in actual life. He saw TT separately for a few minutes before calling me in. I walked into a spacious office with tall windows. The floor creaked under the carpet with each step. He shook my hand before offering me a seat. The fact that there was another lady there with a notebook and pen in hand made me think this was serious.

He looked at me and smiled. "Don't be nervous – you're not in any trouble."

I nodded.

"Can you please tell me about last night's events?"

I took a big gulp as I tried to piece the night together in a way that would keep both TT and me out of trouble and not expose our drinking, since we were underage.

"Uh, yeah, TT and I went to the club, came back really late, and then she went out again to see Tony."

"Who is Tony?"

"He's from the basketball team, sir."

"I see."

"Did you go with her? Did you see her boyfriend that night?"

"No, after she asked me to leave her dorm room, I went straight to my room for the rest of the night."

"You know about the allegations? Miss Tyler is saying some boys took advantage of her."

"Well, I wouldn't really know. I didn't see her until the next morning, I—"

"Isn't Miss Tyler friendly with the boys on campus?" the dean's assistant jumped in.

"I guess." I regretted the words as quickly as they left my lips. The assistant rolled her eyes and went back to writing on her notebook.

"You know, she's been in trouble before for this sort of behavior. You seem like a good kid; I'd keep my distance if I were you," the dean said as he walked me to the door. "You're free to go." He waved for TT to go back in.

Did I say the right things? Maybe I could have done more? I hope she told the same story. After a half hour, I stood up when I saw TT walk towards the door. I grabbed the books she had left on the bench next to me.

"So?"

"Thanks a lot for having my back!" she said while snatching the books from my arm. She turned around and stormed back to our building and slammed her dorm room door behind her. I tried sending her a couple of texts with no response. We never spoke again after that day. I had my doubts about whether she was really gang-raped; TT is a free spirit, but I'm not sure she would go that far. I didn't go upstairs with her that night, I'll never really know what happened.

Arrangements were made for me to move into the all-girls dorm, and TT moved off campus. The vibe with the basketball team felt very different, so I put some distance between them and me. My new roommate, Mia, was very nice. She was a timid girl who had lived in Livingston, Mississippi all her life and mostly kept to herself. I could tell she had been invisible in high school and also in college, because I often introduced her to people who thought they were meeting her for the very first time, but Mia would tell them they'd had science together for two years in high school or were in PE together. They didn't pay attention to her enough to recall ever seeing her; I could tell this frustrated Mia a lot.

Although TT and I had completely lost contact with each other, people still associated us with each other, and soon after the laundry room incident, rumors started going around about me. People were saying I was up there with TT that night and also had sex with the basketball team, that I was on a video, and you could see me having sex with guys. My popularity on campus quickly turned sour. I was embarrassed; I wanted to go somewhere and hide. Everywhere I went, people were whispering about either TT or me.

I tried my best not to let it get to me and to go on about my business, but it made me want to cry. I felt like I was in high school. When I got to the dorm room, Mia only made it worse by constantly telling me of the rumors she was hearing about me. I don't know if she meant to, but I felt like she was rubbing it in my face. One day in my marketing class, a boy noticed me trying to hold my tears back, and so he started speaking to me. He eventually invited me to come over and hang out in his apartment off campus. At first, I had my guard up but noticed that he wasn't like the other boys I had come across. He genuinely wanted to hang out with me and get to know me. The more we hung out, the more comfortable I got with him. We would study, watch movies, and a few times I slept over in his bed while he took the couch. He was my escape from campus life.

Diamond, who could always tell when something was wrong, had a long conversation with me. She told me to stop worrying about the rumors and that all publicity is good publicity. "You're definitely special if people you don't know spend their time talking about you. Believe it or not, they most likely want to be you. So own it! Once you do this, people will quickly lose whatever power they had over you."

I always loved talking to Diamond; no matter what was going on in our lives, we always made time for one another, and when one was in trouble, we would address the issue thoroughly and try and come up with solutions. I got off the phone with Diamond feeling stronger than ever. I started walking around campus with my head held high once again.

Mia was furious when she saw me come into our dorm room with a smile. "Do you not hear what people are saying about you?!" she asked.

"I'm not deaf. I hear them, and I feel special. I don't know half of these people's names, yet they spend time out of their lives to think about me and talk about me – I feel like a celebrity," I answered. I'm not sure if it was my new outlook about the situation or if people had moved on, but the rumors stopped after a while. Things were falling back into place.

17

MY BIGGEST COLLEGE FAN

During the summer, I kept in touch with various people on campus via Facebook or text. I continued to get friend requests from boys who wanted to be my boyfriend and would tell me how pretty I was, and I'd message back and forth with them. I wasn't particularly interested – I was just bored and enjoyed the attention.

One boy, named David, eventually caught my eye. He seemed to be the biggest fan of them all. He had yet to set foot on the campus and had already heard of me from his cousin in Mississippi who went to some of the same pageants I did. He consistently messaged me and wanted to get to know me. We chatted the whole summer and started calling each other every day.

I came back to campus the Sunday before Sophomore year officially started. As soon as Dad drove away, I met up with Gregory at his place. We played video games for a couple of hours while catching up. He invited another guy, Eric, and I invited Slim to come join us. Gregory was preparing drinks for all of us and I noticed his and Eric's cups were large and filled with dark liquor while Slim and I had skinny cups with pink, girly cocktails.

"Gregory, why don't we have the same drinks?" I looked over his shoulder while he was mixing everything.

"Because, little one, you can't handle the other drinks." He looked back at me and smiled.

"How dare you?" I pushed him and laughed. "I can handle your drink."

"Sev, I've seen you drink. You can't handle your liquor, sweetheart." He handed me the pink cocktail. "And besides, this is a grown man's drink, and y'all ain't ready for that."

Slim and I sneaked a few sips of their drinks when they weren't looking, and next thing I knew, I was crawling on the floor because I couldn't see straight enough to stand. Gregory came, put me on his shoulder, and set me down on the couch. "Sev, I told y'all you're not ready for this grown man's drink. I'm switching you to water from now on." He smiled and handed me a cup of water with a bag of Doritos. Between the two of us, it felt like Slim and I inhaled the chips. Gregory drove us back to our dorms to sleep it off.

Waking up the next morning for my first class was extremely painful – everything hurt and I felt nauseated. I usually attempted to dress up for class, but that morning I just wore some sweatpants and a hoodie. I threw up in the bathroom minutes before walking into my art class, where I pulled the hoodie over my head and lay my head down. The teacher called on me to answer a question, but I felt like

I was dying, so I just looked at her in the eye as I shook my head no and laid it back down on the desk. I spent the rest of the day going back and forth to the bathroom between classes.

I felt much better the next day and walked out of the dorm room like someone ready to take on the world. "Wow, you're even prettier in real life!" I stopped and looked back.

"Excuse me?" I asked.

"It's me, David," he answered.

I scanned him from head to toe to jog my memory. He was a tall, thin man with dark brown eyes. His wide nose was the only indication that he might be black; it turns out he was mixed. He was the product of a one-night stand his Mom had with a white man.

"David! Hey!" I happily gave him a hug.

"I wasn't sure you remembered me." He laughed nervously.

We picked up right where we had left off that summer. He began walking me to some of my classes, then taking me to the movies or out to eat. After a week, he asked me to officially be his girlfriend. I thought it was slightly hasty but welcomed the change of pace. It seemed like nothing had changed between us – David would leave me to my own devices during the day as he hung out with his friends. He came to my dorm when Slim wasn't there, or I would go to his dorm and spend the night. I was okay with this for the first three weeks until I blew my lid one day as he was coming over to stay the night. I told him I didn't want to do it anymore because I didn't see the difference between the two of us being a steady booty call and being boyfriend and girlfriend. I told him I felt unappreciated. As I yelled at him, he was really quiet and just looked at me attentively. I wasn't sure if he would just break up with me then and there, thinking I'm too needy.

"Okay, Sev, I understand," he said quietly before leaving to go to his place.

He came back the next day asking for another chance and promising that things would be very different, and I agreed to take him back.

Over the weeks I appreciated the effort he was making towards our relationship. We began spending more time together, and I felt I could trust him. One day he asked me where I saw myself in five years, and I broke down and told him about my dilemma, about how I wasn't able to get any scholarships, that I wasn't sure I'd make it through the rest of the college years. He said nothing; he just hugged me as we walked back to his dorm room to sleep.

I came to my dorm after hanging out with Gregory one night, and I found David waiting for me, mad and jealous that I was spending time with one of my guy friends. We got into an argument, during which he yelled, "I hate it cause I love your ass!" Taken aback, I didn't know how to respond.

"I love you, Sev," he said in a softer voice. I looked at him, confused, as I made my way to the balcony for fresh air.

Does he really mean it? I closed my eyes as the wind caressed my face, almost taking my tears with it. Startled as I felt something touch me, I turned around to see David behind me.

"Can we talk?"

I nodded and turned back around.

We talked for a couple of hours about us as a couple. I had told him about how we were illegal immigrants and that I was not sure could finish school and he would tell me about his childhood. We had many days like this. One night we were up talking about the future. It was three in the morning, and we had been sitting in a gazebo near his dorm for hours chatting, until he eventually went into a monologue. My eyes were becoming so heavy I had to close them for a few seconds before mustering the strength to open them again. He didn't seem to mind. He kept talking about what he wanted our Future to be like, even though he had to shake me awake from time to time. "Let's go to bed," I said, slowly getting up with my eyes opened just enough to see where I was going.

"Will you marry me?" It was as though someone had splashed a bucket of ice-cold water on me, because I was suddenly wide awake.

"What?!" I turned around and stopped.

He grabbed my hand, pulling me closer to him. "You said you didn't know how you would finish the semester, and you can't get any scholarships. If we get married, you can then apply for your green card; What do you say?"

I tried to pull my hand away, but he intertwined our hands instead. "Sevie, I know this is sudden, but I love you and will take care of you."

"Okay."

"Yeah?!" he asked excitedly, double-checking that he'd heard right.

"Yes, I will marry you, David."

With very little sleep from the night before, we began looking for a place to get married and booked the first available date just a few weeks away.

I went home that weekend and waited for both Mom and Dad to be in the kitchen. "So my boyfriend, David, and I were talking and he wants to help me with my papers; we are going to get married." I clinched my eyes closed waiting for a bomb but to my surprise they just looked confused.

"We are working on getting you your papers," Mom answered.

"You guys have been supposedly working on getting my papers for years but nothing has come about,' I answered.

"If you just wait, we can say you were born in Haiti, because it's too hard to get your papers as a French person and get you a social security number," Dad replied.

"Guys I don't want to get regularized this way. I don't want this based on a lie and besides, David and I love each other,"' I answered as I walked away, surprised they did not fight me more on this. In fact, they did not mention it again.

Things were good between David and me; it was almost as though we hit our honeymoon stage before the wedding. On a fine Tuesday morning, David, his roommate, and I walked to a council to meet a pastor to get married. "You're babies!" she exclaimed as she opened the doors for us. "You sure you want to do this?" she asked, concerned. We both nodded, so she walked us to the room where we would get married. She instructed us to hold each other's hands and look into each other's eyes as we repeated after her. *What am I doing?!? God, I'm so sorry – please don't be mad.* The sound of my heartbeat was so loud that I couldn't hear anything else. My eyesight turned to tunnel vision, caving in on itself while I pinpointed a random spot on David's forehead. As though they were leaves caught in the wind, my hands were shaking uncontrollably. I was waiting for God to strike me down at any moment.

"I now pronounce you man and wife; you may kiss the bride." I looked at the pastor for guidance.

"Go on," she smiled as she pointed to David with her head. David leaned over to kiss me, and just like that, we were married. There were no friends, no family, just the two of us, and I preferred it this way, especially because I was not entirely sure of what I had just done.

Antoine came over to us with a gigantic smile. "I wanna take you guys out for breakfast, my treat!"

"That's really sweet, Antoine, but I have a presentation in my accounting class worth 20% of my final grade and—"

"It's not every day you get married, Sev; let the man take us out for breakfast," David interrupted.

"Fine, let's go," I answered, trying to put on a smile. We went to a nice restaurant and had pancakes. I thought about how long I had prepared for the presentation and how well I knew I could have done, but I didn't want to make David mad. We went back to his dorm, and David began looking at various petitions I would need to fill out to get my US paperwork in order.

18

NUMB

Shortly after we got married, David stopped going clubbing or to the gym with friends. He went to class and came back to the apartment, focusing all his time and energy on us. He asked me to move into his apartment, but instead, I moved a large portion of my clothes and all my makeup and called it a day. For a while, I didn't mind his new behavior. Although I knew he expected me to do the same, I wasn't ready to do that. To meet him in the middle, I cut back on time I spent with my friends.

I would see Slim from time to time in my old dorm room. We caught up on everything, watched movies, and hung out. She had started seeing one of my friend's cousins and was not in the room that much, either, but we remained close. My popularity hadn't dropped, people were still hitting on me all the time. I even had someone standing outside my dorm room a few times playing love songs on his stereo like in movies. When I first announced that David and I were together, most of my guy friends were disappointed and had no problem expressing this. When David and I walked on campus together, a couple of people said things like, "He don't know what to do with you." I just brushed it off, but he got angry.

David demanded I no longer sit with anyone in the cafeteria unless he was there. He said I was too friendly with people. I waited an extra half hour to eat lunch with him and his friends one day, hoping this would be a regular thing. "Guys, this is Sevie," he announced as we both sat down.

"Wow, she fine as hell!" one of his friends yelled out. "She looks exotic! Where you from?" another friend asked.

"Nah, nothing special, she's just another southern girl," David answered.

"So, I was born in Paris, France, and moved here when I was ten," I answered while shooting daggers at David with my eyes. They were all amazed. I spent the rest of lunch answering their many questions and telling them what life in Paris was like. While David's jaw clenched tighter by the minute; I enjoyed watching him grip onto his fork until the veins in his hands were showing. He eventually cut off all his friends off and talked to his roommate, Antoine.

Thanksgiving came, so David and I spent a night over at his mom's place. I knew he told me he was rather poor, but I did not know to what extent. His mom, who is a counsellor at the college, drove us to a large trailer a few miles away from campus. I had never been inside a trailer before, but this was definitely a large one. The kitchen and living room were one open space with dark blue carpet and light brown walls. In the back were three small bedrooms and a bathroom overlooking the forest. Between the three sisters and their kids, there was only so much space to move around. All the women in David's family, including his younger sister, had their kids during their teenage years. "Look how happy my sisters are with their kids. I want us to do the same and have kids at a young age," David said to me while watching the kids run around in the trailer. I looked at him like he had two heads.

"We are too young, we have not graduated yet, and we don't even have $2 to our name!" I replied. We argued about it back and forth, but there was no convincing me. That night when he thought I was asleep, I noticed him poking holes in our condoms, so I made an emergency appointment with the campus nurse to get on the pill when we got back to campus.

The next day Dad came to pick us up to go home. I was surprised at the way Mom and Dad had taken the news when I announced we had gotten married. I had explained to them that this could also help as far as citizenship paperwork went and that I did love him. Looking back, there was not much they could have done, since I told them only after I had done it. No matter our family's financial situation, Dad always insisted that we live in a house. He told Mom that this would set the tone for anyone trying to marry his daughters, so they would know what they needed to live up to. They proudly showed David around our house; even though we had two extra rooms, they wanted him to sleep on the couch downstairs while I slept upstairs in my room, out of respect for them.

Diamond and Porsche came over the next night. I introduced them to David, and we were all talking for about a minute before our inside jokes started coming out, leaving David out of the conversation. I got up to get a glass of water, and when I turned around, Diamond, Porsche, and Bridget were standing behind me. "Why aren't you with your man, Sevie?" Porsche asked.

"I'm going there now, Porsche," I answered while laughing.

"You need to be sitting with your man," she replied in her playful voice. Suddenly, the three of them ambushed me and proceeded to pull my shirt down. With my bra out, they pushed me to David, who was sitting on the couch minding his own business. "Here's your woman, David – we prepped her up for you!" Diamond said while laughing. The four of us were laughing so hard we were in tears, while David looked out of place and mildly disgusted with me.

"So these are your friends?" he said as he watched me rearrange my shirt.

"They're more than friends; they are family," I replied while wiping my tears of laughter. He was uncomfortable and felt out of place, but I didn't care. I was just happy to be there, back in my element. The weekend went by quickly, and before we knew it, we were back at UWM.

I was getting ready to go to class one day, going through my routine of showering first, then doing my hair. I was about to reach for my makeup bag when I noticed it was missing. I looked around the bathroom before going over to shake David out of his sleep. "David, have you seen my makeup bag?"

"Yeah, I took it," he casually replied while yawning and stretching.

"What?!"

"You wear too much makeup, so I took it."

"Give me my damn makeup bag!" I yelled and put my hand out, waiting for him to hand it over. He grabbed my wrist hard and looked into my eyes while clenching his teeth.

"Take your ass to class. You're going to be late." Shoving my wrist back, he turned over and went back to sleep. Unfortunately, he was right. I had to get to class, so I grabbed my books and slammed the door as hard as I could on my way out. I felt insecure throughout the day, barely looking anyone in the eye, thinking I was ugly.

I sat in my technology class looking out the window when Blue sat next to me. "You should smile more," he said.

"Oh, hey, long time no see!" We hugged quickly.

"What's wrong Sev?"

"Oh nothing, just had to leave the house with no makeup today," I said while looking away. Blue touched my shoulder to make me face him, studying my face for a few seconds. "Well, could've had me fooled. You still look good."

"Aw, thanks," I replied with an enormous smile. That made my day; I felt like my super-confident self again. I came back to the apartment feeling good and didn't care about the makeup bag anymore.

One evening, Antoine wanted to use the bathroom, but I had just started washing up, and David needed to pee, so I let David come in. After he peed, he jumped in the shower with me. At first, I thought it was romantic and practical for us to shower together, but David liked it so much, he wanted to do it every day. He even started following me to the bathroom when I had to pee or poop. He wanted us to spend every minute of the day together; he was becoming obsessed. This quickly became exhausting, so I opted to go home one weekend, alone.

When Dad came to pick me up, David walked with me to the car, and as soon as we started driving, he called me. I quickly got off the phone with him. It was just Dad and I in the car, and though we didn't have a relationship where we would talk a lot, I still didn't want to speak with David. Utter quiet was the better option.

The last time I had been home, I left my room looking like Hurricane Katrina had hit it; to my surprise, I opened the door to a spotless room with a fresh perfume on my dressing table and a brand new pair of pants lying on my bed. I had originally picked my room because of the vast amount of sunlight, and that day it was brighter and sunnier than ever. Mom would always wash and style my hair when I came home, and this time was no different. I came home with a gigantic pile of dirty laundry and looked like I needed to be put in the washer myself, but after one weekend in Georgia, I was brand new again. I could always count on Mom to make the weekends special by taking care of me.

While my mother was braiding my hair, David called me about seven times. I called back, thinking someone died, but it turned out he wanted to hear my voice. He wanted me to stay on the phone with him for hours, even if we weren't talking. At night he called repeatedly and insisted we stay on the phone until the morning. Dad drove me back to UWM Sunday afternoon.

"Did you have an enjoyable weekend?" David asked.

"Yeah, it was nice. I got to spend time with my sister and Diamond and Porsche. Mom did a splendid job with my hair, see?" I turned my head from side to side for him to admire.

"I was out here looking stupid," he replied. "I don't want you going home without me anymore. If I can't go, you shouldn't go either." I didn't feel like replying and possibly getting into an argument, so I pretended not to hear.

We sat down later that day to look at what I needed to get a visa. "I think there is a way we can do it for people who have yet to start college," he said.

"That's nice, except I'm already on year two, so let's look for the options for that." I looked at him as if he were a madman.

"Yeah, but you could just start school over – just sign up again and do it with my last name." David was one year behind me, because I was about six months older. Sometimes I suspected he had an issue with me being slightly older than him and ahead of him in school. I completely ignored him and kept looking for documents that matched my current situation better.

I struggled with my math class, so at the beginning of the semester, I spoke to my professor, Mr. Mitchell, and asked about any extra practice or one-on-one study I could have. Pleased that I had taken initiative, he set appointments for us to study and review any formulas I needed help with. I went to his house on campus and stayed for as long as necessary. Mr. Mitchell also gave me exercises to do at home, which I didn't mind; it was vital for me to pass that class. College being expensive as it was, Mom and Dad wouldn't be able to afford for me to retake math if I failed, so I had to do whatever it took to pass.

I was studying one night after having left Mr. Mitchell's house while David was watching TV. "Why are you studying so hard?" I could already hear the irritation in his tone.

"Remember I told you about how bad I am at math? And how I take longer to understand everything? Well, I have to practice so I can keep up with everyone," I answered with my head still buried in my book.

"You need to be here," he replied, getting more irritated by the minute.

I rolled my eyes at him "I'm sitting inches away from you."

He sprang up from the bed, snatched the pencil from my hand and slammed my book shut.

"You need to be here with your husband," he uttered through his teeth, gripping the pencil so hard it broke. I got up and went to bed without saying a word.

We lay there quietly, watching football. I felt his hand caressing me – my arm, my breasts, moving down to my hips, and very slowly pulling down my shorts. I grabbed them and pulled them back up.

"Not tonight, I'm on my first day of my period, and my cramps are very strong right now." He let out a long angry sigh while turning to his back. "Sorry," I muttered. He turned to spoon me again, and I fell asleep.

Suddenly, I was being turned from my side to my back. Chilly air grazed against my skin as both my shorts and panties slid to my knees. Sleepy, I tried to reach for them, but they were then at my ankles. Still adjusting to the light, I opened one eye halfway and saw my panties and shorts on the floor. David was sitting up on his knees between my legs. His frigid hands were almost painful to the touch as he spread my legs apart. He came a little closer, squeezing my bare nipple with one hand while stroking his penis with the other. I was certain I had been wearing a top when going to bed earlier. I pushed his hand off my breast. "David, I'm having terrible cramps," I uttered while wiping my eyes.

"Shh, just let me get on top," he whispered as lay on top of me.

"Don't, it's rea—" I inhaled sharply, like I had just jumped into cold water, now wide awake as the piercing pain surged through my body. The potent smell of blood caused me to look down; he was brutally thrusting in and out of me, his eyes blank as though his soul was missing. He was like a man on a mission. I tried to push him off, but he kept stroking, placing his shoulder on my mouth to keep me quiet. Feeling helpless, I managed to wiggle my head to the side. All I could feel were the salty tears coming from my eyes, going across my nose, and into my ear. I didn't want him to see me cry.

He pulled his penis out, and blood gushed out of me like a garden hose, sprinkling on the wall a little before going back to normal. The pain came bolting back but with claws this time. He rolled over onto his back, exhaling deeply before going to clean himself up. I pivoted myself to the side with one hand on my stomach, attempting to ease the agonizing pain. Breathing only amplified it, so I stopped and only took short, controlled breaths when necessary.

"You look beautiful," he whispered in awe while taking a picture of me with his cell phone.

I was screaming on the inside. "David, can you please give me the meds on the table?" I asked while trying desperately not to breathe too much.

"Oh, yeah." He shook his head out of his trance and went to the kitchen. He handed me the glass of water then slapped my ass. I was in pain; he could see it and yet was mesmerized by me. He carefully removed the bloody sheets, making sure not to move me too much in the process, then put a blanket on my naked body. "Here, this is for you," he whispered while handing me a tampon and gently kissing me on the forehead. I guess that was his way of apologizing for what had just happened. I wanted to punch him but there was not much I could do at this point; powerless, I took it and tried to go back to bed.

19
BREAKING POINT

I felt like something had been taken from me, like I had been robbed. I became more reserved and kept to myself. In the cafeteria, I would now just sit alone. After classes or even in the main courtyard, I once talked to everyone and anyone, partaking in jokes, but now I just attended class, kept my head down, and headed straight back to the dorm after.

Things between David, Antoine, and me were messy. Antoine found himself a girlfriend and was rarely in the apartment, yet this didn't reduce the tension. I came back from class one day to find the place sparkling clean, as though we were moving out. The suitcases I'd brought over when I moved some of my things to his place were next to the closet in the bedroom. David was carefully inspecting the now mostly emptied closet. I stood next to him and noticed that most of my clothes were gone.

"What's going on? Do you need me to move my stuff?" I asked.

"I'm just moving all of the clothes I don't think you

should be wearing anymore," he replied while continuing to inspect the remaining articles of clothing.

"What are you talking about?"

"The way you dress, it's too provocative. Take this dress, for example." He took the dress off the hanger and showed it to me. "It's too tight and too short." Looking at me as though I should understand, he balled up the dress and threw it into one of the two opened suitcases.

I went back to get it. "You mean, the dress I wore on our second date, the one you thought I looked gorgeous in? *That* dress?"

"Yeah, we're together now, no need to dress up so much. You're drawing too much attention and are always trying too hard." He yanked it out of my hand and threw it back.

"Look at my sisters, they are always in pants and a T-shirt; they only dress up for special occasions, and they don't even wear high heels like that."

"I am not your damn sisters!"

He came up very close to my face, staring at me, clenching his fist, and breathing heavily while backing me up to the wall.

"No, you're not. You're always trying too hard and trying to be something special. Well, guess what? You're nothing special – you're just another girl, and you need to start acting like my damn wife." He punched the wall inches away from my face just as my phone rang.

"Hello?" I tried my best to keep it together, but my voice was shaky. Diamond was on the other end of the line. I pushed David away from me and made my way to the balcony. He grabbed my arm, but I pulled away as I continued to speak with Diamond.

"You sound shaken, all okay?" she asked.

"Yeah, I'm good," I answered as I looked over my shoulder and my hands uncontrollably shaking.

"How was your day?"

"It was good, let me tell you about this hilarious moment we had in Marketing class." I replied. Diamond knew me well enough to understand I was not okay. She was not the type of person who would force information out of me. Instead, she let me come to her when I was ready and would always try her best to help any way she could.

We stayed on the phone for about twenty minutes; she kept me laughing and giggling. My hands had stopped shaking. With every chuckle I let out, David's teeth clenched tighter. He joined me on the balcony with his arms crossed, staring right at me; I turned in the opposite direction, paying no mind and chuckling even harder with Diamond. "Get in the house," he snapped.

"Hey, is that David in the background?" Diamond asked.

"Huh? No, it's no one, don't worry. What were you saying?" I replied.

"Get in the house," he said a little louder. I turned, rolling my eyes at him. As I walked past, I burst out in laughter inches from his face at one of Diamond's jokes. "Get off the damn phone!" He slapped me across the face, flinging my flip phone shut and across the room. Before getting the chance to react, he pushed me to the floor. I looked up, and he was standing over me, shouting, pointing, his face now strained and eyes dripping with spite. Suddenly, my friend Jay burst in and punched David. He happened to be in the courtyard and saw what was happening. Jay pinned him against the wall by the throat.

"Don't ever touch her again." He punched David again and knocked him to the ground next to me. "If you know what's good for you, you'll stay down." He knelt to meet me eye to eye. "Grab your stuff. You're leaving." I nodded as he helped me up. I grabbed the few outfits left in the closet and put them in the suitcase David had left open while Jay picked up my books. We got into his car and drove to my dorm room, where he sat me on the bed and pulled up a chair to face me.

Since we'd met, I'd always had a crush on Jay, which I suspect he knew, but nothing happened between us. We became such excellent friends that I settled for his friendship instead. That day, all the feelings I thought were put away came back. He was my knight in shining armor, my hero.

With a napkin in hand, he gently wiped my tears. "I noticed you changing since the two of you got together. I was concerned but had no idea it had gotten this bad. I'm sorry I wasn't there earlier."

"You're here now, Jay; that's all that matters." I slowly came closer to him, puckered my lips, and closed my eyes but instead of his lips, I felt his hand on my chin. I opened my eyes confused.

"Sevie, I love you. You know that, right?" I looked at him and nodded.

"You've been through a lot tonight. Why don't you lie down and get some rest? I'll get the stuff out of the car." He gave me a kiss on the forehead and helped me lie on the bed before leaving to get the rest of my belongings.

There were only two days left before the Christmas break. I saw a couple of missed calls from David, which I ignored. The few moments I wasn't studying for my finals, I spent with Jay until Dad came to pick me up. We decided that since the Christmas break was long, and I might have to change dorms for the new semester, I should just take all my belongings. Little did I know, this would be the very last time I'd set foot on the UWM campus.

Coming home felt different from the other times, there was no big fuss; it was as though I'd never left. One night I heard Mom and Dad talking in the kitchen.

"We could try to cut back on the groceries? Or cut the cable" Dad said.

"We don't eat that much, and Bridget does need some sort of entertainment." Mom replied.

I came downstairs with a letter from school.

"Guys, I can take a semester off, or two." I said, wiping

my eyes and yawning.

They both turned to look at me, surprised.

"Look, you've already re-mortgaged the house, Mom works almost three jobs, and once you've finished paying for me, Bridget will be right behind."

"Are you sure?" Mom asked.

"You forget I'm the one that helps you translate all of the bills and helped set up the direct debits. I know how much money goes in and out of this house too." I replied. "It's the only option for now. Besides, this letter from the school says I'm not allowed to start another semester without clearing the balance first."

"Okay," they both said.

"I will try to look for a job in the meantime." I stated as I left the letter on the table and headed back to sleep.

Guess I won't be seeing my friends anymore. But on the bright side, I won't have to see David again; he can't get to me all the way in Georgia.

20

TIME CARRIES ON

During this time, I kept in faint contact with David, who told me several times he would come live in Georgia until he got me back. He would beg for me to come back and when I didn't respond to such advances, his tone of voice would quickly change and he would become verbally abusive and bring me to tears. I was far from him yet still within his grasp, I hated him and loved him at all once. Although I never told them all of what had happened, Diamond, Porsche, and Bridget were my support system, and with their help I cut the calls with David short, until I stopped picking them up at all. We never did file for the marriage license so the marriage had cancelled itself out and I was finally free of him, but I still had to pick up the pieces of my heart.

Mom harshly reminded me every other day of the fact that I came home early from college and got married. It hurt, but I brushed it off; I was happy to be home; I had escaped the toxic college situation.

The school semester was over for me, but not for

Diamond; she and I had started school two weeks apart, with me being first. Since I had nothing better to do, I went to classes with her sometimes. Kennesaw State University has classroom sizes so large that no one ever questioned my presence. After her class we would get something to eat, or I would wait for Lamar, who also attended Kennesaw, to come pick me up and go to his house for a while.

I got myself an interview as a housekeeper in a Days Inn. It didn't pay much, but it was close to home. The management didn't check my paperwork and eligibility to work in the country, so when they offered me the job, I took it.

"I start tomorrow, only because the lady who will train me had to go home early," I exclaimed, as I got in the car where Mom had been waiting for me.

"That's good." She responded without so much as a glance. "Try to come home with a paycheck and not another husband this time."

The next day I got home from work and it was just Mom and I in the house. We watched *Oprah* while waiting for Bridget to come home from school. Out of nowhere she turned to me and shouts.

"How could you!"

I looked at her confused. *What the crap is happening* I asked myself.

"You know you have ruined your life, right? YOUR LIFE IS RUINED! You're nothing but a failure" she continued.

I didn't want to say anything, I did not know where all of this had come from.

"You came home from school and got a husband! For all I know you got yourself pregnant which I honestly wouldn't put past you since you're so crazy and naïve. DO YOU KNO—"

I couldn't take it anymore, so with my throat tightened and my lips quivering I rushed upstairs to my closet where I quietly sobbed and remained there until Bridget came home.

I had nightmares about what had happened at school and during the day, the torment continued but now Dad had joined in. This continued for a while until I finally snapped. I wanted it to stop, to shut her up for good, so while Mom was in my room, standing over me and telling me of how much of a failure I am, I bolted to the kitchen and looked for the sharpest knife I could find. I turned around and she was right behind me.

"I'm nothing but a failure! I've ruined my life right!" I shouted with tears spilling over my face like a river escaping a dam. "So then why should I deserve to live if I'm as bad as you say? I might as well kill myself." I closed my eyes, holding the knife up with both hands, taking a big breath in as I hurled it towards me but I felt a force stop me. It was Mom; she squeezed my hand, forcing me to drop the knife and as soon as it dropped, she kicked it across the room. I dropped to my knees sobbing.

"You said I was nothing, so why not just let me die then?"

Mom quickly got on the floor, hugged me and whispered, "You're okay, you're not a failure."

Bridget took the liberty of calling in sick for me. From that day on, my mother never bullied me like that again; I would get the occasional jabs, especially from Dad, but not as bad as before.

The housekeeping job started pressuring me about my papers, so I had to quit. I looked for things I could do by correspondence or online, but everything required paperwork which I could not provide.

The winter holidays ended and Bridget and Porsche started school again, and eventually Diamond went back. With each passing day, hopes of ever setting foot back on UWM campus slowly withered away. Every day at home was the same; I would search for jobs online, then watch daytime television. At times I sat by the window and watched the world go by, wondering what was to become of me.

21

PRAYING ON HER HANDS AND KNEES

Bridget and I never really saw it, but Mom and Dad were having problems in their marriage. Mom would hear rumors about Dad's behavior at work towards women, or she would find condoms in his car. His infidelity kept him from being around as much as he should be for his family. To keep up with the house payments and my college bills, Mom had taken on three jobs. She worked at Chick-Fil-A, at the WellStar Hospital, and occasionally at a school. Mom took a lot of pride in the way she looked, and after running around, making sure we had everything we needed, she sometimes had no time to eat, and when she ate, it would be unhealthy food. She no longer had time to take care of herself. One day Mom woke up before the alarm rang and started getting ready for her 6:00 a.m. shift at Chick-Fil-A. Driving down the road, she noticed the road was unusually clear, with no cars. *Strange*, she thought to herself while parking her in front of the restaurant.

With sleepy eyes, Mom waited for the manager, Tim, to come and open the restaurant. Fifteen minutes passed, and she began wondering if she should call him and check if everything was okay. She pulled out her phone and looked at the clock. Twenty minutes had gone by when she realized it was 3:00 in the morning. Mom drove home and dragged her feet back up the stairs. As she pulled the bed sheets onto her Dad turned over to her.

"Didn't you notice I had gotten up from bed at 3:00 a.m.? Why didn't you say anything?" she whispered.

"I wasn't sure what time you started work," he answered, shrugging.

"Yvon, I've been working the same hours there for three years."

"I don't keep track of your hours – good night!" he responded.

Seeing there was no use in arguing, she went back to sleep as the time to get up again was coming fast.

When she came home to take her Chick-fil-A uniform and put the WellStar uniform on, I noticed that she was tired.

"Are you ok?" I asked as I passed her by in the hallway.

"No, didn't you notice I was up at 3 last night!" she shouted.

"No sorry I was asleep Mom," I replied defensively.

She told me about her night and how she had woken up too early.

'Oh, that sucks,' I replied

"Never mind, no one cares anyway," she mumbled as she made her way downstairs and into the car.

Dad eventually got himself a job at WellStar Hospital like Mom. There he met a woman named Miranda and began having an affair with her. On the days he was off and Mom was working, he would leave for hours at the time, come back with a single jug of milk and claim to have been out doing the groceries all this while.

Mom began hearing the rumors at work and shortly after found the condoms in his car which she brought up to the room one day.

"Why are you doing this to me?" she asked, holding the wrapper up.

He swiftly glanced at her before going back to what he was doing. "I needed a change, something new," he replied.

"But I'm your wife," she pleaded.

"Yes, yes, and we've been together for so long now, I need something new." He could tell she was fighting back the tears. "We done here? I'm going to make myself something to eat."

Unbothered, he went downstairs without looking back. Within the Caribbean community, people are very traditional, and things like divorces are rare. The men are almost praised for their infidelity while women are forced to accept it to avoid the humiliation of divorce. Mom was discreet concerning her dirty laundry; they were a perfect match, with Dad being such a private person himself. She liked to keep up the appearance of the perfect family. Between the two of them, they did a wonderful job hiding all of their marital problems as Bridget and I had never seen nor even heard them argue for more than five minutes. Their marriage was hanging on by a string, and Bridget and I knew nothing of it.

Devastated, Mom went into her closet and fell to her knees, squeezing her hands together while breathing heavily from the heartache. "God, please help me! Please get me out of this trap. I can't go on any longer; I'm at the end of my rope," she begged. She knew she had to refrain from making too much noise; she didn't want Bridget or myself to hear but I was in the next room and heard everything.

"I need you to save me from this now. I can't go on any longer! Lord as you are my savior, I'm begging you, please—"

"Mom! Can we go out? I need some lip gloss," Bridget yelled out.

Mom wiped her tears and quickly got up, fixing her face in the mirror before going downstairs to Bridget. I waited until she came down the stairs to get out of the guest room just across. I didn't want them to know I had heard everything; it was the type of conversation I wanted to avoid at all costs. They never spoke to us about their marriage, let alone the tumultuous times they were in the midst of.

Despite what Mom was going through, it had to wait. She knew she had to dig deep to gather the strength to keep going. She had to find the fortitude to keep being an excellent Mom and a dutiful wife.

22

SUNDAY BRUNCH

Every Sunday, we attended a church called Trinity Chapel. Dad had stopped going to church with us after a while, so it was just Mom, Bridget, and me. We discovered Trinity Chapel shortly after moving into the house. It was one of those mega-churches you see on TV that looked like a small castle on the outside. They had two Sunday services packed with 1,200 members at each. The church had three floors with enormous screens on the main floor and a series of smaller screens for the other floors. We tried our best to get there early enough to get a seat on the main floor by the ushers.

The service always kicked off with this random lady screaming at the top of her lungs "Haaaaallleeeluaaahh!" I never knew where she came from and never even saw her, but I imagined she was black and on the heavy side, possibly in her fifties as such women have the most powerful voices. Her Sunday scream would be the cue for the drums to start, the strobe lights to turn on, and people to clap to the beat of the music.

Professional artists who knew how to get the crowd moving sang catchy worship songs. Everyone got into it, dancing their hearts out. People in wheelchairs would spin around like crazy, others ran up and down the aisle singing at the tops of their lungs and raising their arms up to the Lord, while Mom, Bridget, and I got down with Jesus. Walking into Trinity Chapel in the mornings, you couldn't tell the difference between a church service and a night club. By the time we got to the actual gospel of the day, we were out of breath and wiping the sweat off. I always looked forward to going to Trinity Chapel – it was always so much fun, and this particular Sunday was no different. The preacher rapped well for a white man.

Mom told us that Oncle Evens was coming over with his kids to have lunch with us. Hurricane Katrina had turned their house in Florida to dust, so they used their insurance money to move to Georgia, into a much larger home than the one in Florida. They visited us from time to time, but apart from Pierre, there was a sizable age difference, making it more of a chore to hang out with Oncle Evens's children than anything else. Bridget and I always ganged up on the baby brother who was awkward and a mama's boy. The last time they'd come over, she and I barely paid any attention to them. I felt bad and took it upon myself to make sure they would enjoy their stay in our house this time. When they arrived, I greeted them at the door and led them upstairs to play video games. Not long after, Mom called us all downstairs for lunch. The table was covered in a new silver cloth I hadn't seen before; on top were the fancy plates and our new silverware. It looked beautiful and was paired with exquisite food – a salad, then rice and chicken, and for dessert, she had made her famous strawberry sorbet, which she made only for special occasions like Christmas or a birthday. Unsure why it was so elaborate, I was thankful – thankful for them all, for this wonderful Sunday lunch, the beautiful day outside, all of it. They went home late that day, and I went to bed in a great mood.

"Severine! Severine! Viens!" I thought I was dreaming until the hallway light turned on and forced me to open my eyes. I trudged out into the hallway, wondering if I'd really heard Dad's voice or if I was dreaming. I looked around and saw him downstairs.

"Come on, they took your mother," he exclaimed. "What?"

I asked while trying to wipe the sleep from my eyes.

"The cops, they came and took your Mom," he answered. "Come help me look for her ID so we can try to get her out. Wake your sister up," he instructed. I pulled Bridget from her bed. We went into their room and got a change of clothes for Mom while Dad got the paperwork he thought she would need. We got into the car and drove to the nearest jail, where Dad thought she would be. He parked, and I unbuckled my seatbelt. "Don't." I felt Dad hold me back.

"Why?" I asked.

"Because you may also be on Immigration's radar, and they may take you in if you're not careful," he replied.

He and Bridget got out of the car and disappeared into the building for twenty minutes before coming back.

"Where is she?" I looked to the both of them for answers.

"They've sent her to a jail in Florida," Bridget responded.

We drove back home. Dad made a few phone calls before getting ready for work, and Bridget went back to bed since she had school in a few hours. I lay in my bed but didn't sleep. Instead, I called Lamar in tears, and while he empathized with me, there was nothing he could do, nor was it his responsibility to do something in the first place. When I told Diamond, she realized all she could do was tell me everything would eventually be okay.

Later that day, Oncle Evens came by the house again. We never really talked, so it surprised me to see him, but I assumed he heard the news and wanted to see if I was okay. We drove to McDonalds, where he asked about the family and how we got to the US, and I told him what I knew. He said I was on the US Immigration's radar since I had sent in an application off to them and that what happened to Mom was very unfortunate. Since Mom and Dad put in a different application for Bridget, she was safe for now. We drove back to the house, and right before I got out of the car, he looked straight into my eyes and said, "You will have to go back to France." I looked away for a second. *This is my home now, I grew up here... but then again, I'm not doing anything in this country anymore. I can't finish school, nor can I work. Heck, just the other day I asked God what was to become of me, and maybe this was it. Maybe I am supposed to go to France and hope for a better life there.*

"Okay. If that's what it takes, then that's fine," he was taken back by how quickly I accepted my fate.

23

THE LAST DAYS

No longer feeling that Bridget and I were safe, Dad sent us to his brother's house. I let Diamond and Lamar know that we were staying with Oncle Will. It was fine because Willson and Farah enjoyed partying most days, so it was like being in a nightclub all the time – especially because they would invite their friends, whom Diamond was already familiar with. Willson planned to throw a large get-together before Christmas. He wanted everyone to wear black or red, hired a venue, and gave out invitations to all of his friends and a few random strangers he saw in the streets. Diamond and I were excited. It wasn't like we hadn't gone to parties before, but we had to dress up for this one. We went out to the mall to look for the perfect dresses, got our hair and makeup on point, and made our way there. We drove to Atlanta, finding ourselves in a medium-size building, which was too large for the number of people there. It wasn't at all decorated, but there was a photo booth and a photographer and splendid music. It came as no surprise that not a single one of the strangers

Willson invited bothered to show up. Overall, the party was okay, but there was a discrepancy between the amount of hype and what it turned out to be.

My birthday came, and Lamar wanted to take me out. We went to a house party and watched some fireworks before heading back to his house. He had bought me two bottles of white liquor. Because it was my twenty-first birthday, I thought it would be symbolic to have twenty-one shots in twenty-one minutes.

We made it to his bedroom in the basement where he lined up a couple of shot glasses for the both of us. He got the timer ready, and we got started; we got to shot number eight when he stopped to go to the bathroom. As soon as he turned around, I took two more shots. I felt fine for two minutes, but then the alcohol hit me like a ton of bricks. I must have blacked out, because when I opened my eyes next, we were having sex. My eyes and when they opened again, and we were on the floor, watching TV, but I was sobbing; begging God to make sure Bridget would be okay. Although I was trying to stay positive about going to France, I was terrified at the idea of Bridget being on her own. I was her big sister; it was my job to look after her, and it was going to be tough to do this from an ocean away. Surprised, Lamar didn't know what to do, so he hugged me until I stopped. I closed my eyes and opened them again and looked at him. "I've got to pee," I declared. Lamar looked back at me, confused.

"Okay." He shrugged, wondering what he was supposed to do. *Why is he just standing there? Is he going to watch me pee now? What a weirdo.* His eyes widened as the yellow liquid flowed out of my body.

"Sev, are you really peeing right now? You're freaking kidding me, right?" he asked, annoyed.

I didn't know why he would ask such a stupid question after I'd told him I had to pee. I looked around and realized I wasn't sitting on the toilet seat. In fact, I wasn't in the bathroom at all; I was sitting up on the side of his bed, peeing in my clothes and on his bed. *No wonder he's mad.*

I closed my eyes and opened them again. He was on the phone with someone. "Yeah, your friend almost threw up on her cell phone. She's really out of it right now – she even peed in my bed!" He turned to look at me. *He must be on the phone with Diamond.*

My head was too heavy to hold up, and the room was spinning, so I laid it down and closed my eyes. When I opened them again, I was in fresh clothes and felt well rested. I showered and brushed my teeth before calling my Tante Farah to come pick me up. Lamar told her what happened that night, which pissed her off. "You should have thrown up in his bed while you were at it; he shouldn't have gotten you so drunk!" she exclaimed while driving us back to the house.

Christmas day came. With Delphine's death, we barely celebrated Christmas most years. Mom was still gone, Dad was almost never around, and Bridget and I were like orphans over at Willson and Farah's house. Oncle Will came into the room where Bridget and I were staying and gave us each $20. He wished us Merry Christmas before walking away. We looked at each other and smiled. We were grateful he thought of us in the first place and happy to be with each other during those times.

Will and Dad bought me a one-way ticket to Paris for January. We hadn't renewed my French passport, which had expired when I was fifteen. Since we had planned on settling in the US, it was not a top priority, and now it was too late to have it ready in time for the flight. We made an appointment with the French Embassy in Atlanta and asked them for a *laissez-passer* ("let them through," a transit permit). They gave us two copies, one to be given to passport control in Atlanta and the other to passport control in Paris. The only thing left to do was wait out the days. I tried to get excited at the idea of going back to France, tuning up my French, and having a better chance at life that didn't involve dodgy paperwork, yet another part of me was also heartbroken. I realized the sad feelings I was pushing down came out when I drank, which explained the outburst at Lamar's house. I decided never to let myself drink so much, never to show anyone how sad I felt on the inside.

We were able to contact the church regarding Mom's case and convinced the US Immigration to send her to Haiti instead of staying in jail waiting to be deported to France.

Dad kept advising us to write Mom a letter. Bridget had, but I never even took the request seriously. Before I could even put pen to paper, they had flown Mom to Haiti.

At the Port-au-Prince airport, her older brother and my godfather, Oncle Roness, greeted her. Oncle Roness had been a fashion designer in Canada who had just gone through a nasty, expensive divorce. He had listed the home he and his ex-wife had lived in for sale, and finally a buyer appeared, just in time to pay the legal fees for the divorce. The buyer gave him a check for $250,000, which Oncle Roness deposited in the bank. Two hours after the check cleared, he tried to withdraw this cash, only to find that the government had spotted it and helped themselves to the money he owed in back taxes. The account was wiped clean, and they left him with nothing but a letter from the government saying, "Thank you for your payment." Angry and broken, he used his last few dollars to book himself a one-way ticket to Haiti and never looked back. This turned out to be a blessing for Mom, because she had someone to greet her at the airport, especially since she had now become a tourist in her own birth country.

With one week left to go before my flight to France, I got a call from my stepsister, Carlene. She had been calling for a few nights, asking Dad if I could stay with her in Paris. They had originally planned for me to stay with one of Dad's childhood friends, Clarel, who was also Bridget's godfather, but I guess Carlene's constant calling and crying wore Dad down, and so he finally agreed to have me stay with her instead. Oncle Will came into the room that night and handed me the phone. Carlene told me I would be staying with her when I came over to France. All I could do was agree. The only time I had seen Carlene was at Delphine's funeral. I didn't know much about her at all, just that she was weird, clingy, and always smelled somewhat musty. I tried to stay positive and looked forward to having an older sister again. After nine years, you kind of forget what that's like.

Bridget and I moved back into our house; Dad felt it was safe again, and I had to start packing anyway. Diamond stopped by to help. When she arrived, I barely said hello. "See the boxes over there? See if you can put them in the suitcase," I ordered. She didn't respond. I could see on her face she was mad, but she quickly understood that I was just frustrated with the situation and my lashing out had very little to do with her. Like a noble friend, she got to work and hugged me goodbye on her way out. Later that night she came by with Porsche, Ebony, Porsche's best friend, and Ivena. Dad was asleep upstairs, so we remained downstairs in the living room. They had sold some of the furniture, so there was extra space. He was trying to save money, so we couldn't turn on the heat, but it didn't bother us; we gathered in a circle and kept our jackets on. We played Uno, a simple game, but when we got together, it always felt like the best game in the world. We filled the night with tears of laughter; it was one of the best nights of my life, and it was the last time we would ever be like this.

The next day I got my suitcase zipped up and ready. Diamond stopped by one last time to give me a very long goodbye hug. I dragged my suitcase downstairs, and Dad told me to be careful. It was super heavy, but I didn't care. I would not be carrying it around – boys would help me, I assumed. As he was packing the car, Dad gave me $500 in cash. I immediately called Bridget to give her some money. "I thought I would go with you," she said. "It would have been so cool, just the two of us in Paris."

I looked at her and smiled. "Yeah, that would be great, but guess not."

I sat in the back with Bridget as we drove to the airport. We went through some of the security checks together without saying a word. I came to passport control and gave them the laissez- passer. I was about to turn around and say goodbye to Bridget and Dad, but the officer shoved me into the line. I desperately looked for their faces, but the line kept piling up. All I could see now were strangers. I tried to poke my head between people and give a wave, the officers told me to keep moving. With no way of turning back, it dawned on me that this was it. I turned around, facing the line, and held my breath so that the tears wouldn't come. I thought I was about to faint; knots came into my stomach, so I started to take small and controlled breaths. This was not the time nor the place to cry. Like everyone else in the line, all I could do was move forward and pray to God we would all be okay. Little did I know, I wouldn't see my father and sister again for another five years, and this was the very last time I would ever see Dad standing up.

24

VIVE LA FRANCE!

I focused on maintaining a positive outlook. This was the beginning of a new chapter, a chance to start over. I knew the language, even though my French was that of a ten-year-old and very rusty, since I only practiced it with Mom and Dad. I was going back to my home country. No more was I to be an alien, so why not embrace this fresh adventure?

The plane landed, and I was back in the immigration queue. I handed the officer the second copy of the *laissez-passer*; he nodded and pointed me to the exit. Somehow my suitcase, when I collected it, felt heavier than before, forcing me to take frequent breaks. I desperately tried to make eye contact with guys in hopes they would help me, but no one even looked at me. Suddenly I saw a tall man walking right up to me. "Ahh, it's heavy no?" He pointed to my suitcase.

"Yes! Really heavy," I answered, relieved, while stopping to relax my hand and wait for him to take over. Instead, he just laughed and walked right past me. *Welcome to France,* I thought while gathering the strength to take the suitcase on again.

I came out of the terminal and started looking for a person who would somehow recognize me. The last time Carlene and I had seen each other was nine years before at Delphine's funeral. I'd grown a lot since. Would she even recognize me? Would I recognize her? I made eye contact with someone who smiled back and started walking towards me.

It was Carlene. She looked like an older, tired version of me. Her skin was greasy with little makeup, her hair was unkempt, and she wore mismatched clothes that didn't flatter her body. Her oversized coat had a few holes in it and was zipped halfway up, forcing her to constantly re-adjust it on her shoulders. You could see at first glance that she'd had a tough time and had taken a beating by life, but her pretty smile showed she was strong. She had come out of it alive.

She greeted me with kisses on both cheeks and introduced me to her guy friend, Luke, who immediately took my enormous suitcase. We drove from David de Gaulle Airport to her house in a city called Sarcelles. The lengthy drive gave me a chance to look out the window and take it all in – the unique buildings, the compact cars in the tiny roads, how the people looked and dressed – everything.

We arrived and parked near her apartment building, and although I had never seen her place, it was exactly as I had remembered the projects in France. These buildings, called the Habitation à Loyer Modéré or HLM, are houses or apartments given by the government to people who can't afford to get a place on their own. We walked into the high-rise and took the elevator to the tenth floor.

We bumped into Carlene's next-door neighbors, The Abdoula family, who introduced themselves. They were a family of five with a Mom, a Dad called Mohamed, two sons and a daughter named Fatu. Fatu was around my age and friendly. She invited me to come sometime, which I accepted before turning back to Carlene.

As Carlene opened the door to her apartment, she turned back with a smile to see my facial expression; I tried my best to hide my disappointment. There was a small, dark kitchen with dishes piled up in the sink. I could see small roaches in the corners but stayed composed. Bugs terrified me, and roaches grossed me out more than anything, but I rushed in and out of the kitchen as she was giving me a tour, pretending it didn't bother me one bit. She took me to the living room, which had a large plastic table and chairs. There was no TV, but there was an old green couch in the corner. We went into the hallway which was the only part of the apartment that had some light thanks to a tall black lamp. She then introduced me to my niece and nephews, who all slept in one room with a bunk bed and a twin bed. Tom was the eldest of the three and only a year younger than Bridget. Carla was twelve, and the youngest one, Gregory, was eight. I put my hand out to say hello, but they all insisted on giving me a hug. They were my nieces and nephews, after all.

"You'll stay with me in this room." Carlene pointed to the room just across from the kids. It had an extensive wardrobe and a queen-size bed. The apartment was in Fifth

Arrondissement, which is a considerable distance from the city center; still, you could see the Eiffel Tower illuminating the sky, and even in the compact, gloomy room I was standing in, it was magical and brought me comfort.

I had just about enough time to change my clothes before Carlene called us all to dinner. We ate and made small talk. She told the kids I was here to take care of them and to help her because she felt overwhelmed. I didn't know why she said that, nor did I argue; I just kept telling my stories of my life. The meal came to an end, and all three of the children got up. Assuming they would take their plates to the sink, it bewildered me to see them turn their plates over on the table, letting the spaghetti sauce stain the white plastic table and fall onto the floor. Never in my life had I seen anything like it – especially not from a black family. Carlene sat at the table with her head down. "What's going on? Why are you letting them do this?" I asked.

"Oh, you know, kids are just kids. You can tell them to clean up," she answered. Even though these weren't my kids, and I had arrived in their lives just minutes ago, I couldn't just stand by and watch.

"Hey, guys, would you mind picking your plates up?" I said as I followed them to the hallway. They looked at me and nodded. They walked back to the living room, took their plates to the sink, and even cleaned up their mess.

As we both got in the bed, she admitted to me that the kids had overwhelmed her for some time. Shortly after she divorced her abusive husband, he turned the kids against her, and there was not much she could do about it. She told me she was happy that I'd come to help her out with the children. She knew nothing about me, let alone my situation. I was only twenty-one years old, nowhere near ready to take on such enormous responsibility. Besides, my niece and nephews hadn't met me until now. Who was I to tell them what to do in any way, shape, or form?

The next day, Carlene introduced me to one of her friends, Josie, who lived nearby. "Josie, come meet my sister, she's here to help with the kids!" I looked at her, annoyed, but didn't want to cause any problems, so I just introduced myself. Josie was also in her late thirties also but different from Carlene. We went to her apartment, which has the same layout as Carlene's but better furniture. Josie was the type of woman who took care of herself, and you could tell. She told me to load up my résumé, and she helped me convert it to a French CV.

Later that week, we sent it off to Disney, where Carlene worked. She had been working there in housekeeping since the park opened in 1992. Disney quickly called me in for an interview, and they hired me on the spot. After doing an all-day orientation, I was assigned my position and given my official start date.

"What position did you get?" Carlene asked.

"Field entertainer," I answered while reading the letter. "Oh, I get to do the official opening of their new attractions, the Tower of Terror!"

"Wow, auntie, you're so lucky! I've been seeing commercials about it all week," Gregory exclaimed.

"No, no, no, you're supposed to go for something like a waitress or maybe a housekeeper like me," Carlene answered as she took the letter from my hands. "It's an easier job for you, trouble-free, not like this one. It's too complicated."

"Well, let's see how it goes." I shrugged. "It might be fun."

"I'll go talk to them and see if you can change," she answered, rolling her eyes.

25

GETTING ADJUSTED

I paid no attention to what Carlene said. She held no weight at Disney. She had been working at the same job for a little less than two decades without ever moving up the ladder nor a pay raise; she was stuck in the same spot, doing the same thing. To me, this spoke volumes about whatever influence she thought she had with Disney's upper management. Still, I was thankful she helped me find a job, and I tried my best not to show off my new position too much. A few days before my first day at Disney, I went to work with her to get a gist of the route. The long journey made me forget the initial reason I even got on the train. I was happy to have a big sister look after me; Lord knows it had been a while since I'd had this.

I made the trip again on my own. After all, we worked in different departments, and therefore we most likely wouldn't have the same schedules. As I boarded, I told myself I would take the train to a single station, then come back and take it from there. Nervous, I realized this was officially the first time in my life I'd taken the metro alone.

When alone, you really notice how long it is between stops. I got off at the first stop, but when I tried to turn around, there was maintenance going on, forcing us to shuffle in a one-way formation to the street. By the time I got out to the street, I was a five-minute walk away from the station, and I didn't know which platform I should stand on to go back. All the metro maps were unclear to me, because I didn't know how to follow them.

Panic came over me as I searched for any familiar landmark with no luck. *What do I do now?* I asked myself as I frantically looked around. It started raining. I tried to use my rusty French to stop anyone who would speak to me and ask where the metro station was, but people were too busy trying to escape the rain to pay me any mind.

Not knowing my left from right, I felt the tears coming to my eyes. In the crowd, I spotted a tall, olive-skinned boy with black hair, walking around with his hands in his pockets and unbothered. Everyone was running away from the rain as though the water were harmful, yet he looked like he didn't have a care in the world. "Are you lost?" he asked. I was so busy staring, I hadn't noticed he was walking up to me. I nodded while wiping my tears. "Okay, so where are you coming from, angel?"

"A place called Sarcelles, but I don't know how to get back," I answered.

I felt idiotic and as helpless as a child. Being in a foreign country when you barely know the language makes you feel that way. Back in the States, when people see foreigners struggling in the day-to-day life, they assume they are stupid, when in fact, it's a simple language barrier – one that can make or break you. I wondered, at any point, had I ever looked down upon an immigrant? Of course I was one while living in the US, but my English was too good for anyone to notice after six months. Now more than ever, I knew the feeling; I knew what it was like to be helpless and having to put my complete trust into this stranger, hoping he would take me home.

Without so much as the address, we walked back to the train station and headed over to Sarcelles. "So, uh, how long did you live in the States?" he asked.

"Eleven years, but I'm actually French."

"Really?" His puzzled look confirmed that my French accent was bad enough to make him think I was anything but French.

"Yeah, many people thought I was American, but I'm actually French; I'm Severine."

"I'm Akim," he replied as we got off the train and at the Sarcelles stop.

"So, do you know where you are now?"

"Yes, I think so," I said with a bright smile. We chatted while walking back to Carlene's building and exchanged numbers. "We made it! Thank you so much for helping me," I declared while extending my arms for a hug.

"No problem, angel. I got a little something for you." He

took my hand and placed an object in it. "It's a metro map; keep it with you always. It will help you find your way. Oh, and text me whenever you want."

He had a crooked smile but still had a friendly face you could easily trust. He and I texted back and forth, and he admitted that he liked me, but he did so using French slang I was unfamiliar with, so I never really knew. On the days we were due to meet up, he would pick a different place in Paris every time, giving me little clues as to which metro line to take. This helped me get the hang of reading the metro map, and before I knew it, I had the entire map memorized.

Day one at Disney came, and the work did not feel like work – I had so much fun at the Tower of Terror and made friends with loads of people. It didn't matter that Carlene had broken my previous phone; I was filling this one with brand new contacts. There was a fair amount of advertising for the Tower of Terror; ads for it were everywhere – in the park, the metro stations, and on TV. This attraction was not meant for little kids nor the faint-hearted. Everyone talked about the fact that the ride made you drop at the rate of one meter per second. Our team leaders briefed us that the grand opening meant doing late shifts. Disney put this in place to give celebrities and royalty a chance to go on the rides privately. The team leaders arranged the rotation so that everyone did at least one late shift a week. Because this shift finished at two or three in the morning, the company arranged for taxis to take us home at the end.

My niece and nephews were excited and wanted to know how soon they could try this new ride. Each time I mentioned the Tower of Terror around Carlene, she began huffing and puffing before storming out of the room, so I tried not to talk about it so much when around her. I did mention the fact that no one knew the exact time the late shift would finish, as it depended on the day. On the days I worked the early shift, I would come home and then head back out to go hang out with Akim for a bit. We went into Paris if it was early enough, but since sundown was as early as 7 p.m., I didn't want to stay out too late so as not to cause any trouble at the house.

Carlene said nothing to me about Akim, let alone having any issues with him, but she told Dad I was out at all hours of the night with him. I found this out only when I spoke with Bridget. Bridget and Dad called every so often to see how I was doing, and when they did, Carlene would speak with Dad. Then, when I wanted to speak, she would hang up, saying they'd run out of minutes. She did this three or four times before I bought a phone card of my own and went to a payphone a couple minutes' walk from the house to talk.

When we had days off together, she would take me out to see some of her friends. Since she was fourteen years older than me, so were her friends. All the men she hung around with were married, but that didn't seem to stop them making passes at me and yet looking at the floor when their wives were around. I thought it was disgusting that they would even look at me that way considering the large age difference. There were two in particular, Peter and John, who made it known they liked me. They had seen me at one of Carlene's friend's houses, and for whatever reason just kept showing up are our house after that, saying they wanted to help Carlene repaint the apartment. Carlene enjoyed having them around and paid no mind when I told her they kept making passes at me.

One day she scheduled them to come over for the paint job. The hot water in the apartment ran only during certain times of the day, restricting the times we could bathe. It was noon, right around the time the hot water became available.

For the first time since I'd been here, Carlene offered to run the bath water for me. "Go on and get undressed in the room, and I'll let you know when the bath is ready," she said. She turned the water on and went on to the living room to pick up a call. I was about to take my clothes off when I heard her whisper on her cell phone and then heard the front door open. I sat really still on the bed to better listen to what was going on. "Go on, she's in the room," Carlene said. Footsteps slowly approached as though the person didn't want to be noticed. "Heeeyy!" Peter exclaimed as he opened the bedroom door wide. I could see John's dismayed face when he saw me, apparently disappointed that I was clothed. "Oh, hey, we just wanted to say hello since we stopped by and all," Peter explained. John waved hello and went to the living room to join Carlene. I followed them both and took a seat on the couch. Carlene looked puzzled to see me and asked, "Weren't you going to get ready for your bath? The water is almost ready."

"No, that's okay. We have guests now; I'll go after," I answered.

They stayed for another five minutes before leaving. The atmosphere was awkward; neither of them had any painting equipment with them whatsoever. I never confronted Carlene about that day, but I stopped trusting her.

The next day I was on my first late shift. I started work at three in the afternoon and took a meal break at six. The celebrities of the night were rugby players who liked my accent and wanted me specifically to take them into the Tower of Terror's elevator and do the security speech. We finished just before 2 a.m. I was shattered and slept in the taxi on the way home.

When I got upstairs, I noticed there was no need for the key as the door was already open, and Carlene was on the couch in the living room.

"Where were you?!"

"I was working, remember?"

"What do you mean you were working? The park is not open at this time!"

"So, remember I told you about the Tower of Terror and its grand opening week and how everyone on the team has to do the late shift at least once?" I replied.

"I'm telling Dad about this. I'm really tired of you coming home at all hours of the night. Now get to bed!"

Too tired to argue with her, I just got into bed while she stayed behind and slept in the living room. The less I was in the house, the more she would tell Dad I was out during all hours of the night with Akim, but Akim and I hadn't seen each other since I started working, especially since I was getting home later than usual.

I was able to work for Disney using my outdated National ID card, but I still didn't have a passport. Carlene took me to the city council one day. They asked for my birth certificate, which I didn't have. They asked me to come back with that, a proof of address, and Carlene's ID to prove I lived there and that she was my sister. We left with the list of items to gather and a case number for when we came back. I got home and grabbed a pen to see what we could start checking off the list.

"Carlene! Let's get the documents gathered so we can go back as soon as possible. I just need your ID, please, and for you to write a statement saying I live here with you," I said delighted. She stayed quiet for a minute, sitting on the couch and looking out the window, leaving me standing there with pen and paper in hand. After shooting a quick glance at the list, she replied, "I'm not writing anything" and turned her head back to the window.

"Okay." I wanted to ask why but just wrote the statement that I was living in her house as proof of address and came back to her with it written. "Hey, if you don't mind, could you sign this and give me your national ID so I can make a copy to take to the council?"

"No," she responded, "I will take no part of it!"

"Why not?" I answered, trying to hold my anger back.

"Your parents are into some shady activities, and I don't want to be involved. Hell, do you even know if you're French?"

"What do you mean? I was born here," I replied, confused about where all this was coming from.

"Are you? With all the shady stuff your parents did in the States, how do you know they didn't just *say* you were French?"

"Never mind, I'll look for another way," I replied. I didn't want to admit it, but her question haunted me for a while.

Tensions were mounting between us, and me coming home late once a week from work only made it worse. My job had twelve-hour shifts and long commutes, and Carlene was realizing that I wasn't around to take care of her kids; I was there for me. I was always uncomfortable when she introduced me to people and then told them about how I came all the way from the US to help her with her children. She only mentioned me as her sister and never Bridget, as if she didn't exist. Therefore, it came as a relief when the idea of me being there for myself started sinking in for her, and she didn't like it.

Three weeks went by, and she asked me to pay 500 euros for rent. My first Disney check hadn't come through, and even when it did, I needed an ID to open a bank account, which was an issue. Her anger grew when she had to pay for my transportation to and from Disney for the month; even though Disney paid 60% of transportation, it still meant money was coming out of Carlene's pocket. I grew uncomfortable around her, and the atmosphere grew worse. To limit my encounters with her, I requested a certain set of days off that differed from hers, reducing our time together solely to evenings, and even then, she slept in the living room.

She constantly told me she talked to Dad regarding my behavior and how disappointed he was. At one point, she told me he was coming over to France because of me. When I told Bridget, we both laughed because we knew he neither had the will nor the resources to make such a trip.

The money Dad had given me to start my life in France was slowly running out, and with no proper ID, I didn't see how I would be able to even open a bank account to cash the paycheck coming from Disney. On my day off, I went to the city council to see how else I could get proof of residence. The man behind the counter searched for about ten minutes and reported that the file that was opened a few days before had been pulled out and cancelled. My stomach sank, leaving me feeling weak. I wanted to scream but got choked up instead. "I'm guessing you knew nothing about this?" the man asked while looking at me with compassionate eyes.

My voice would be shaky and broken, so I just nodded as tears filled my eyes. "I'm sorry to hear that," he said. "Come, let's get a coffee; you look like you need to talk. I'm Izdime." He grabbed his coat. Without a second thought, I followed this stranger to the nearest coffee shop, where I told him about my experience so far. He focused and nodded.

"So, your sister is well aware that you just need proof of address, which she can help you with but is refusing to do so?" he asked, trying to get a clear picture of the problem.

"Basically," I answered, shrugging.

"Okay, I want to help you. Meet me at the council one week from today. I'll help you open a bank account so you can at least cash the first check when it comes. I've got to get back to work, but don't forget! One week at the same time." He placed a few euros down on the table before grabbing his coat and heading out the door, disappearing into the crowd. On my way back home, I decided not to bother confronting Carlene about this. For some reason, she didn't want to help me. I would have to do it on my own, and I hoped Izdime would help me. It was in my best interest to do this without her knowing about it.

I was down to my last ten euros, and although we had a subsidized cafeteria at Disney, I still couldn't afford to buy food. I started trying to make sandwiches from home with just a baguette, ham, and cheese. There were days when

I was starving, so I'd splurge on a bag of chips in hopes it would hold me over during the twelve-hour shift. I came home from work one night and noticed a baguette in the kitchen. The day had been so crazy, I hadn't had a chance to eat and was starving. I went to the sink to wash my hands and came back to the baguette which seemed to have moved a little. Thinking I was merely tired, I went to reach for it when it moved again; the middle of it was pulsating as though it was about to explode. I blinked slowly and got closer to make sure I was seeing correctly. Next thing I knew, a thin black string popped out of the baguette and then a second one just like it. *The baguette has hair?* I thought to myself, but they weren't strings, they were antennae – antennae from the cockroach that had eaten its way through the baguette. Terrified, I covered my mouth to stop myself from screaming as it came out of the other side of the baguette. I slowly stepped back while watching the cockroach go across the top of the baguette, then around it. No longer was I hungry, for fear and disgust had taken over my body, leaving my hand too shaky to turn off the light on my way out. I never ate in the house again after that. I made do with a small bag of chips for the twelve-hour shifts.

26

OUT THERE IS BETTER THAN IN HERE

The next day I walked back to the council to meet Izdime and found him right outside waiting for me. "Hi, good to see you again," he said while giving me a kiss on each cheek.

We walked to the bank, took a number, and sat down. *What is it he will tell the people at the bank to make it so I can finally open a bank account?* I wondered. Our number got called and as I was about to get up, he gently sat me back down. "wait here, let me do the talking." He walked over there to counter and the man behind smiled while walking around the counter to give Izdime a hug. They were laughing and smiling the entire time they spoke to one another. Izdime then pointed at me and the men made their way over. "Hi, I'm Rick, I understand you're looking to open a bank account with the BNP today?" He eagerly shook my hand.

"Yes, but I don't have a passport, I just have an expired ID card, and no actual proof of address."

Rick looks over to Izdime for a moment before looking back at me "Don't worry about these things, it will all be taken care of for you- right this way." I followed him to a small office where he helped me fill out my paperwork and was told to come back in a few days to pick up my bank card. I walked out looking at Izdime in complete awe. "Wow thank you so much! I tried to do this myself, but it didn't work; how did you do this? And who is that guy?"

"Don't worry about it, he's an old friend. I have a lot of connections in this town, if you stick with me I can show you," he replied with a smirk. He took me to a café to talk. At the risk of sounding ungrateful, I asked him for help with my passport but he explained that this was a lot more complex because I virtually had no documents with me to begin the process especially now that Carlene refused to help me. We chatted for a couple more minutes before he had to go back. While it disappointed me about the passport issue, today was still a big win; I would soon have access to my money.

Over at Disney, I volunteered myself to work late shifts; the later I came home, the fewer chances I would have to interact with Carlene, plus I would get time to get a few things done in the morning prior to going to work. Carlene and I barely talked anymore, and yet the tension filled the air in the house. I needed advice and was unsure exactly who to turn to. When Carlene needed government advice, she would go to a guidance counsellor, so I did the same.

The lady recognized me from the last time I had gone with Carlene. I asked her about housing options for myself and told her I couldn't stay in the house anymore but my plea had fallen on deaf ears; the guidance counsellor had picked sides, and she wasn't on mine. "I think you should go back to your sister," she said while cutting me off.

"but I don't think she has my best interest at heart, I'm not comfortable staying with her and that house is disgusting—"

"Be thankful you even *have* a place to stay, now Ms. Desrosiers I need to get on with my day," she said as she opened the door and pointed me to the exit. I slowly stood up, wanting to cry and to slap her but I realized she would never understand and I didn't know enough French to explain it to her either; so instead I just looked at her as I walked out of her office.

That evening I came home from work and found Carlene waiting for me on the couch. "My house isn't a hotel! If you can't respect that, then you need to get out!" she yelled. She was aware of the reason for me being late, and I knew she saw the taxi from work outside, but I wasn't going to argue with her.

"Fine!" I shouted back, I grabbed my red bag along with a few more items in the closet and made my way back out the door. Fatu's father, who happened to be standing outside, looked at Carlene, confused.

"Carlene God sees everything, he sees what you are doing to this poor girl; you will have to answer to him about these actions one day," It was the first time I had ever seen him angry. I thanked him and pushed the button for the elevator.

Carlene paid him no mind. "Go! Leave! You have nothing, no passport, and you're not going to be anything anyway; not without the help of your sister, you'll see!"

"Sister?" I was about to walk into the elevator but stopped. "I have a sister, her name is Bridget and she lives in the States. You are a stranger who happens to have my last name. Don't ever call me your sister ever again." I walked into the elevator and down the stairs. I called Josie and asked permission to crash at hers. It surprised her to see my big red bag with me when she opened the door. Without asking too many questions, she gave me a couple of pillows to sleep on her couch. Oblivious to what my next move would be, I solely concentrated on the fact that I was going to work the next morning.

"My father will do some voodoo on you if you don't give me my sister back!" awakened by the shouting, I sat up on the couch wondering where that came from.

"You need to give her back! How dare you have her stay the night! She is my sister, not yours!" It was Carlene. She was downstairs shouting at Josie who was in her bedroom window. It had been a while since I had slept until 10am. I opened the living room window and stuck my head out. "Get your ass home right now or I'll call Dad and tell him!" Carlene threatened. I looked at Josie who was panicking over the situation. She came over to me and had my red bag in her hand. Before she even spoke, I knew what this meant.

"This is too much for me to handle, I wish I could help you but I can't get too involved." Although disappointed, I imagine this was not at all what she had signed up for. "Josie, you have done so much for me already, don't worry about it at all. I'm thankful for your help." I gave her a hug, grabbed the rest of my things and headed back to Carlene's apartment. Somehow the place had gotten even darker and gloomier upon my return. Carlene didn't say a word, so I passed her by without saying a word, placed my bag down in the bedroom and got ready for work a couple of hours early. That night I kept tossing and turning in the bed and I knew I couldn't stay, I no longer trusted Carlene, it was time to go. The next morning Carlene told me not to go to work for the day and instead to look into getting her the rent money she had asked me for. I just nodded my head; little did she know I now had a bank account where the paycheck came into and that today was my day off. The moment the door slammed shut, I jumped out of bed and got on my knees.

"God? It's me. I don't feel good in this house and think I need to leave. I need you more than ever. Please stay by my side and carry me on the times things get tough. Just please stay by my side."

With very little to no idea of where I would go, let alone what I would do, I got up and started packing my stuff. At this point, I convinced myself out there was safer than being in this house. I walked over to the kids' room with my bag and in hand and knocked on their door to get their attention. They all looked down at the suitcase for a few seconds. "You're leaving?" Carla said.

"Yeah, I kind of have to do this." I answered with a smile.

"We understand, our Mom is crazy; we were wondering how you lasted this long in the first place." Gregory stated.

I gave them each a hug and walked out the door over to the neighbor's house. Mr. Abdoula opened the door and smiled. "Come on in." He offered me some tea before going to get Fatu for me. I explained my situation to her. She was sad but not at all surprised. "Do you want to stay here?" she asked

"Thanks, but we both know that's not possible; besides, this is not your problem to solve."

"Is there anything we can do?"

"Yes, a favor; Can you please keep this suitcase for me? I'll come back for it as soon as I can."

"Consider it done."

I found a cybercafe, sat down and read emails Bridget and Diamond had sent me to take my mind off of things. After about an hour I left and walked through the flea market. I was lost, I did not understand where to take it from there. I sensed water on my cheek, then water in my hair, on my hand, on my feet. I looked up at the sky; it was raining. At a far distance I saw two officers who I walked up to and asked if they knew where I could find accommodation. They said if I walked at the end of the road, I would find what I'm looking for. They looked like they were in a hurry, as though I was taking precious time out of their hands, so I didn't ask for them to elaborate. I nodded my head and walked on even though I did not understand what they were talking about. My French was probably not good enough for me to properly ask anyway. I walked to the end of the road and sat on a bench in the rain, placed my red bag on my knees and started sobbing. Hearing the footsteps of people passing me was a harsh reminder that the world owes me nothing. I knew this journey would be long and that things would get worse before they got better but I had already started it and therefore there were no other options now other than to finish the journey and see where it takes me. The vibration in my pocket stopped my sobbing. "Hey what are you up to? I haven't heard from you in a while." It was Izdime I felt relieved upon hearing his voice.

"Hello? Are you there?"

"Yes, I'm here. Um, so I run away from my sister's house and have nowhere to go. I'm not sure what to do but can't go back there!"

"Woah woah, ok stop crying; text me your address I'll come collect you."

Knowing that he was on his way comforted me. I tilted my head back towards the sky again, embracing the sprinkles of rain pouring over my face without a care.

Out of the shadows, I saw a figure walking towards me. Until now I had only really seen him in a suit and trench coat so it made me second guess whether it was him when I saw a man in a hoodie and ripped jeans. The second he waved, I grabbed my red bag and ran to him for a much needed hug. "Hey, you ok?" he asked with an empathetic look on his face. I didn't want to cry again so nodded yes. We took the bus over to his friend's house. A powerful smell of weed hit me in the face the moment the door opened. A tall, chocolate skin man with dreadlocks down to his back greeted us with an enormous smile. "How you doing? I'm Noah," he declared while pulling me in for a hug then grabbed my hand and caressed it.

"I'm Sevie," I replied with a nervous smile as I dragged my hand away. The apartment had a nice size living room with a lengthy balcony. The guest bedroom had nothing in it but a queen size bed, but I didn't mind. I went to the end of the hallway to freshen up before coming back out to the living room to sit with the two men. "Do you smoke?" Noah asked while holding his cigarette containing weed.

"No thank you."

"Well can I offer you a drink?" Before I had a chance to answer, he poured me a glass of whisky. I trusted Izdime so didn't hesitate to spill my guts out and explain the entire story. Both men listened without saying a word. "I'm sorry to hear that you ran away," Noah said while taking a sip of his drink.

"So, you don't have anywhere to go?" Izdime asked

"No not really, I don't know many people here in France and since Carlene smashed my first phone, I don't have a way to contact any family right now." I answered. Both men looked at each other and smiled.

"You can stay here as long as you like pretty girl."

"Thanks Noah."

We talked and laughed for another hour before I decided it was time for bed. Both men were so busy drinking and smoking that neither of them noticed I hadn't touched my glass of whisky. I went into the guest bedroom and sat on the bed for a moment, trying to process everything that happened so far.

"Mind if I sit with you for a while?" Izdime asked as he walked over.

"Thanks for doing this. And please thank your friend too."

"You can thank him later yourself." he replied as he leaned over to kiss me. I was uncomfortable, I never looked at Izdime that way. To me he was like an Oncle, I wasn't sure how old he was but if I had to guess I'd say there was at least in his early 30s. He put his hand on my leg and slide it upwards. I put my hand over his to stop so he removed it and gently pushed me on the bed. "Izdime, I can't, I'm sorry. I've got a lot going on as you know and this is the last thing on my mind right now." I sat back up and looked away. He got quiet for a few seconds, then sat back up and pulled my chin over to him.

"Sev, I've done so much for you. I got you a bank card when no one else could, and now I'm giving you a place to stay."

"I know but—"

"How were you expecting to pay for this exactly? I know you have little money."

My heart leaped into my throat as panic surged through me; just like that, the image I had of him was shattered. Behind the sharp suits and the flashy smile lied a monster.

"Look, we're not bad guys here. Just do this with me, then my friend, just to show your gratitude." He stood up and walked towards the door. "I'm gonna take a shower real quick but don't think about this too much okay? We'll go easy on you and who knows, you might like it. Trust me." He left and closed the door behind him. My stomach sank, I sat on the bed for a few seconds, paralyzed. *Ok Sev, this place isn't safe, you can't stay here. Move and do it quickly while he's in the shower.* I snapped out of it, grabbed my bag and coat, then cracked the door open to peek out. I couldn't see his friend but could hear someone on the phone aside from the water running in the bathroom. Standing on the other side of the balcony was Noah. He was arguing with someone on the phone with his back turned so I tiptoed over to the door, opened it and ran out. I ran so fast down the stairs, I'm not sure I closed the door behind me at all. I burst the front doors without looking back and ran into the streets, not seeing the bus that was coming until it stopped inches away from me. "Please let me on!" The driver opened the doors and looked at me up and down. "This is a night bus, going to Paris, understood?"

Out of breath, I nodded and prayed he would go already. I didn't care where the bus was dropping me; I just needed to put some distance between Izdime and I. I hadn't had a sip of alcohol but felt just as dizzy as I usually do when tipsy. My neck hurt from looking back every 30 seconds. I turned back one last time and took a deep breath, cut short with my phone's ringtone. It was Izdime, I quickly put it on silent so as not to bother anyone else on the bus but it kept lighting up so I tried to stop my hand from shaking long enough to turn the flip phone off.

The sun's ray brushing against my face woke me up. I looked around, I was on my own; just me and the driver. Hesitant to turn my phone back on, I had no choice, I needed to know the time. 10am, I had 27 missed calls and another 20 something texts, all from Izdime which I deleted. I walked to the train station and made my way over to work. My shift didn't start for a couple of hours but they had showers and I figured I could just sleep in one of the subsided cafeteria until it was time to start. Hopefully, I could get a bit of time to figure out my next move before the end of my shift that night.

27

AN ANGEL FROM THE SKY

During my lunch break I explained my situation to one of the team leaders, Elza. Elza was an Italian lady who had grown up in Poland and moved to France a little over a year ago. My French improved at a fast speed but my American accent was still heavy. Between the two of us lay a thick language barrier. I finished speaking and paused, awaiting an answer, or a reaction, even a mere sign of life from her. With a blank look on her face, she replied "you have a 50% employee discount should you stay here for a while," and walked off. I wondered if she did not like me or if she felt the situation may be too much for her to handle, but knew I couldn't count on Disney to help. They priced all Disney hotels at around 250 euros a night so 50% off only goes so far when working with a small paycheck.

It was the end of the night and as I waved goodbye to my colleagues, I realized I had nowhere to go. The plan of action? Get on the train and get to the center of Paris; surely the city that never sleeps would offer me more options. The swift ride left me in central Paris in a matter of minutes. Gard-Du-Nords felt like an excellent place to get off the train as it was very central. *Now what?* I asked myself. There were less than 10 other people on this platform as opposed to the usual hundreds during the day, making it seem larger than life. Half of the lights had been turned off; a subtle sign letting us know this part of the station would close soon. *Maybe I can use the little bit of money I've got left to get a hotel!* Although happy with the idea, my stomach hurt at the thought of me having to ask one of these strangers about hotels around here. I dragged my feet and first passed by a callow man looking at his phone. He didn't flinch when I passed him by; staring, hoping to make eye contact while wondering if I should speak to him. I then passed a woman staring out onto the platform; then walked passed a family, and as I made my way towards the very end of the platform, I noticed her. The girl with a hoodie on. She stood in the shadows, bobbing her head to the music which I could hear through her headphones; Her head turned towards the wall. Everything about her body language told me she wanted to be left alone and yet I felt compelled to ask her. I tapped her on her jacket and she turned her head and removed her headphones. "Hi. Um, do you know if there are like any hotels opened around here?"

She looked at me up and down and shook her head no. "There shouldn't be anything open. It's late, Miss."

Gutted, I hid behind an enormous smile, "OK, that's fine. Well, have a good evening." A tap came on my shoulder just before I was about to walk away.

"Wait, do you not have anywhere to stay?" Her face became serious.

"No, I don't. Um, but well, I'll be fine. You, you have a good evening." I waved bye and turned around again. She gently grabbed my arm, stopping me in my tracks.

"Hang on. From one black person to another" She paused for a second and broke the eye contact we had, as though she was going over this in her head before making an ultimate decision. "You can stay with me tonight," she declared.

"Really?" I looked at her eyes and she smiled back with them while nodding yes.

"Gosh, thanks um..."'

"Kelly, and you are?" she answered.

"Sevie."

She and I talked on the train about anything and everything. Life about boys, parents and work. Kelly told me we were headed over to "Saint Denis" which happened to be one of the few places in Paris that I knew a little from faint childhood memories of when we went to the flea market there.

The apartment building was an old white skyscraper in desperate need of a paint job. We got off on the 17th floor and before opening the door, Kelly stopped to look at me.

"You can stay with me, but only for tonight. I need to go to London tomorrow. And I must be there early."

I nodded yes, and she put the key in the door. She opened the door to a cute one-bedroom apartment filled with white furniture. The apartment seemed like the perfect size for a single person to live in. I put my bag in the corner and just stood there looking around as she dropped her keys on the kitchen table and sorted through her mail.

"Kelly, I have to tell you. I like to think I'm a sympathetic person myself, but what you're doing for me, I'm not even sure I would have done for someone else."

She stopped what she was doing to come over and grab my hands "No worries. I can see that you're in need which I'm able to provide," she answered. I had met this girl who seemed no older than me on a platform a little less than an hour ago, but knew I can trust her with my life. Something about her aura or energy put me completely at ease.

"You can put your stuff in the room. Feel free to use the bathroom if you need," she said with a smile.

"Oh gosh, thanks. Don't mind if I do." At the risk of being rude, I took a long shower. It was nice not to have to keep a lookout for roaches for once. The potent aroma of rice and chicken enticed me to finally come out. We ate dinner and chatted some more. Kelly noticed how bad my hair looked so she grabbed a comb and worked her magic. With everything that had been going on lately, I had neither the money nor the time to maintain it.

"Thanks for the meal," I said while yawning and stretching. I dragged my feet towards the couch, I felt shattered with fatigue.

"No, no! you are my guest, go in my room and sleep. I'll sleep out here."

"but—"

"You look like you could use a really good night's sleep." She looks at me and points to the bedroom.

"Thank you so much."

The second the pillow made contact with my face, I went into a deep sleep. By far this was one of the best night's sleep I had in a long time. It was as though all the problems I had were muted for a while just to help me sleep. I woke up feeling well refreshed. We ate breakfast and walked over to the station. My bag felt different and heavy, but I thought nothing of it.

"Honestly Kelly, I'm not sure I would have done this for anyone. I don't know why you're doing this for me and not that I'm trying to scare you, but I could have been a murderer and yet you've invited me to your home."

"You're not a murderer." She laughed. "You're just a girl in need of help, which was a pleasure to provide. It costs me literally nothing to have you stay with me. I'm just sorry it was solely one night."

I stopped and gave her a long hug before continuing to walk to the train station. A thousand thank yous later, Kelly and I parted ways. I got on the train and placed my bag next to me to search why it was heavier all of a sudden. There was a note at the top which I hadn't noticed before.

> *Sevie,*
> *It was so nice meeting you. I've put together a list of numbers and addresses I think can be helpful. I know it's not much, but can hopefully get you further on your journey.*
> *Best of luck!*
> *Kelly.*

She had put together a list of phone numbers and addresses I could call to help get a place to stay and various government help. Kelly also placed a couple of cans of foods in my bag along with a map of Paris. Feeling super thankful, I want to text her and tell her thank you yet again. It was important for her to know that her actions changed my life and that as soon as I got a place, I would treat her like a queen. I took my phone out before I realized her number was not in my phone. I peeked out the window and searched for the white skyscraper I was in last night but couldn't see anything like it. While it was late at night when she took me to her place, still, you'd think one could see a tall white tower in broad daylight and yet it was nowhere to be found and now the train had started moving. *Had I made all of this up?* The note was definitely there and the canned foods were real. Perhaps God sent me an angel from the sky and her name was Kelly.

28

HELL, PERSONALIZED

I started going through the list of hostels and cheap hotels Kelly had given me. I tried to choose some on the way to work, but it proved complicated – closer to Disney, there were fewer hostels, but farther from Disney was closer to Paris, which was out of my price range. Neither the hostels nor the hotels had vacancies for more than a few days, so I was always on the move. During my break at work, I would call to see if they had space and if so, I made a reservation. The lockers Disney provided were big but not big enough for all of my stuff, so I had to go back to the hostel where I'd stayed the night before to collect my bag and then to the new hostel, with little to no idea of the distance between the two places.

Sometimes this transaction was straightforward, and then there were days when I worked overtime, felt shattered, and was then greeted by snow at the end of the long workday. Still, I was thankful to have a roof over my head. On super busy days, when I didn't have much of a break or there was no availability anywhere, I ventured out onto the snow looking for an open train station so I could put my bag down and rest until the morning.

Lucky for me, I realized night buses take hours to get to their final destinations, and I knew if I took two buses, I could easily get up to six hours of sleep, which was enough for me. I made sure to sit very close to the driver, assuming he could help me should anything happen. This became my Plan B when I was unable to find a place before the end of the workday. On such days, I went to work early to shower, and then I slept in one of the cafeterias until the start of my shift, hoping my red bag wouldn't be too much of an issue. The times I used this strategy left me feeling exhausted before I even started working.

My turn for the late shift came around again. After getting in a lot of trouble with the team leaders for using my phone on the job, I didn't dare take it out again. I had dropped my things off at a hostel on Kelly's list earlier that day, but I needed to call and tell them I would come in late that night.

At the end of the shift, Gus, Mehdi, and I hopped into the Disney taxi. The three of us had known each other since orientation and had become friends. Gus had just turned eighteen and was looking for something fun to do before heading off to college. Mehdi was in his early twenties and was still figuring himself out. I had a small crush on Mehdi when we first met – right until the moment I met his boyfriend. Our friendship went only so far because we didn't work on the same attraction; we only saw each other during our breaks a couple of days a week. Gus was the first one to get dropped off, and I was next. Having trouble finding the place, I called the hostel, but it was two a.m., and the staff had gone home. Unable to see clearly, I could not pinpoint the building where the driver was meant to drop me off. We circled around for another twenty minutes until Mehdi said, "Just stay over at my place for the night."

"You sure?"

"Yeah, it will be fine and much easier for all of us," he replied with a smile.

I felt so relieved. Our friendship had not gone far enough for me to tell him I was homeless. I had attempted to tell the team leaders, but I didn't want everyone to know about it, nor did I want anyone's pity.

Stepping into Mehdi's house was like stepping into Marrakech. The furniture was all red and gold, with different intricate patterns on each piece. Fragrant oils scented the entire house. We headed to his room, where he gave me his bed and slept on the couch next to me. "If you need anything, I'm right here," he said, grinning, and then he turned the lights off.

The next morning, his Mom greeted us with breakfast, which we ate in his room. We chatted for a little longer, and then I was on my way again after a shower. *I've got to choose hostels that are open all night.*

I went back to the hostel and secured the room for two weeks; it was only fourteen days, but I was happy to have some level of stability, no matter how short the term. Moving on a day-to-day basis was so stressful that I hadn't even looked around before giving the manager my money and making the reservation. It wasn't until she gave me the receipt that I noticed the holes in the wall and how dark the hallways were. We went up the creaking steps to my room on the fourth floor, which was no bigger than a broom closet. I had a small wardrobe, a twin-size bed, and a large window which allowed me to see the flea market below. Only a few traces of white were left on the dark yellow walls. Cheerful nonetheless, I unpacked my red bag and placed what I could on the dusty hangers.

On my days off, I went straight to the city's offices to try to get a passport. Mom had warned me about the French administration system in the past, and sure enough, each time I made an enquiry about my passport, the list of proof and paperwork only got longer. They asked for my birth certificate, proof of address, Mom and Dad's marriage certificate, passport photos, my family book, and then some. I was running around Paris like a headless chicken, going from one location to another trying to collect the various documents. I often found that getting one – like my parents' birth certificates, for example – meant filling out two other forms and waiting a couple of days or sometimes weeks.

To recover from all of the waiting in long lines and filling out forms, I sometimes sat in a cybercafé for a couple of hours with a hot chocolate. I read emails from Diamond and Bridget and surfed Facebook. When I could, I got some phone cards to call them on my cell. Unfortunately, I could get only about an hour's time on a cell phone vs. 1,000 minutes using a landline or a payphone. On the days when it wasn't too cold, I would grab my largest scarf, put on my gloves, and go to the payphone a few minutes away from the hotel to call them. Walking in the cold streets of Saint Denis, I had no idea of what was currently happening in Hiram Georgia.

"Dad, I'm not doing this with you!" Porsche yelled.

It was a typical Saturday morning in the Williams family. Porsche had asked her Mom to take her to Walmart to buy some tampons, but just as she was about to leave the house, she realized she'd left her wallet inside. Amid her search, she got into yet another argument with her Dad, Jerome.

Jerome was an ex-soldier who became a cop immediately after leaving the army and picked up a drinking habit somewhere in between. Paired with his anger issues, it didn't take him too long to become violent. He and Porsche had similar personalities, causing the two of them to bump heads often, especially now that she was getting closer to being a legal adult. Their arguments became part of the weekend routine. Wanting no part of it, Diamond started working Saturday mornings to get away from the family for a couple of hours.

"Oh, so you can talk back now?" Jerome shouted back from the living room. Porsche rolled her eyes and kept looking for her wallet in her room. Agitated that she hadn't answered, Jerome rushed down to the garage and grabbed his gun.

"I'll show her," he muttered to himself while making his way over to her.

"What did you just say to me, little girl?" Porsche looked up to see her Dad standing in the doorway of her bedroom, pointing the gun at her.

She was scared but remained unfazed. There was no way that she would give him the satisfaction of reacting. Nonchalantly, she walked towards the door without so much as a glance in his direction. He clutched his handgun, now boiling with anger, and pushed her back.

"Nah, nah! Repeat what you done said earlier." He widened his stance, fully blocking the exit.

"Dad, you're being crazy right now. Let me through." Porsche pushed her father out of the way, but he shoved her back, much harder this time. She reached for the gun and attempted to wrestle it out of his hands, but he fought back. A loud bang stopped them in their tracks. They glanced into each other's fearful eyes for a split second before looking down. The blood sprinkled over Porsche's shoes. She looked at her hand, which was on her stomach, and saw nothing but blood going through it. A stinging feeling brought her attention to the lower left side of her stomach. A bullet had fired, and it had gone through her hand and into her stomach.

"You shot me! You actually shot me!" she screamed. Terrified by his action, Jerome dropped the gun and slowly stepped back, finally getting out of Porsche's way as she limped out of her room with her hand still on her stomach. Though she grew weaker with every step, her overwhelming determination to make it to the end of the hallway and into the kitchen kept her going. With bloody hands, she reached for her phone and called Diamond.

"Hey, Porsche?" All Diamond could hear was wheezing. "Porsche, are you okay?!"

"Diamond? Something happened to me," she muttered, "and it's bad, but know that I will make it okay. You'll see – I'm gonna get out of it."

"Porsche! Porsche!" Without thinking twice, Diamond made a U-turn to rush back home.

Unable to hold herself up any longer, Porsche fainted and fell into a pool of her own blood. Floyd, the girl's brother, had been in his room the whole time and wondered what the noise was all about. He opened his bedroom door to a horrific scene. Blood stained the walls, and Jerome sat on the floor, staring vacantly at nothing. Panic-stricken, Floyd took a big gulp and followed the trail of blood leading to the kitchen. There, he found Porsche face down in the blood, unconscious. "Mom! Mom! Call 911!"

In a Paris cybercafé, I was surfing on Facebook and saw a picture of Porsche on Diamond's wall. The caption read, "I squeeze her hand. And she can squeeze back. This gives me hope."

Puzzled as to what Diamond was referring to, I glanced over to the window. It was already dark. Saint Dennis was one of the most dangerous areas in Paris, not a place one wanted to be at night. I started typing a message to Diamond and stopped in the middle of it. *Be a good friend and go call her instead of sending some Facebook message.* I grabbed my scarf and jacket and headed to the payphone.

"It's Porsche. She's in the hospital."

"Oh my gosh!"

She explained everything to me. She told me about how the cops and news media came and filmed Jerome coming down the steps of their house with a bloody shirt and the gun in his back pocket. She told me how her extended family called her and told her to say it was all an accident, never even asking if Porsche had survived.

That incident reinforced what I already knew. Diamond always knew exactly how I felt when I had drama with my family. She was never really surprised at the crazy stories I told her; her family was just as chaotic as mine. I listened and empathized with her. Like the great friend she is, she then turned her attention to me.

"Sorry, Sevie, I've been talking about my drama this whole time and didn't think to ask about you. How are you doing?"

I smiled, thinking what a wonderful friend she was. We

were the best of friends, and I wanted to tell her about my own situation. I wanted to tell her about the nights I had spent in the streets, how Izdime reacted when he found out I was homeless, everything – but now was not the time, for we were each going through our very own personalized hell.

29

WHATEVER IT TAKES

"I'm fine," I replied, "so do we know when Porsche might wake up from the coma?"

Diamond explained to me they had high hopes that she would make it. I called Bridget as soon as I hung up with Diamond.

The news of Porsche had hit her just as hard as it did me. Dad and Bridget were never close, but Bridget told me that living in the same house with each only other brought them a little closer. They lived together as roommates, side by side.

"I started sobbing as soon as Diamond told me the news. The weirdest thing is, Dad passed by my room and asked what was wrong; when I told him, he didn't dismiss it nor make snarky comments about how they are a messed-up American family." She paused. "Instead, he sat next to me and hugged me for a while."

Wow for the first time in a while, Dad was being compassionate, a side of him I always doubted existed.

"I'm surprised but happy." I responded.

With growing concerns for my safety talking on a payphone in a dark alley, I hung up and jogged back to the hostel.

Each time I saw the hostel, I noticed how ancient and rundown the place was. The bathroom had small holes in the walls and a dodgy lock. It was peculiar how the manager's husband always seemed to have to work on something or other near the bathroom every time I went for my shower. I avoided taking a shower there and did so at Disney, but I didn't have much of a choice on my days off.

Every day, I went home and went over the list of documents I needed to obtain my passport and set out to look for a way around the missing pieces. Almost every step required a birth certificate, and because you have to fill out a form and get a copy that is valid for only so long, I walked around with three copies of it in my bag at all times. Without my old passport, even proving I was French was an ordeal.

On the list of numbers and addresses Kelly provided was a government organization that helped people with proof of addresses and accommodation. When I got there, they asked me a few questions then gave me restaurant tickets and an address I could provide the council as my official proof of address. *Another small win!* I now had an address I could use but was still missing the family book and Mom and Dad's marriage certificate, giving me any proof that I am French. Dad didn't have the documents, and I didn't have any contact with Mom, who was in Haiti, the last I heard. I looked at my bank account, and it became clear I couldn't afford to stay in hostels much longer; my expenses outweighed my paycheck. Before the fourteen days were up, I had to find a solution.

While at the cybercafé one morning, I saw another message on Diamond's wall suggesting that Porsche was awake. Without a second thought, I bought another calling card, grabbed my scarf and jacket, and headed to the payphone. Porsche was still in the hospital, but she was awake with Diamond and Bridget by her side. Diamond and I were now sisters, and Porsche was, with Bridget, my other little sister; our foursome was back in business. Bridget told me that when she first saw Porsche, she had to fight back the tears, but then Porsche took out a titty, and they were back to cracking jokes and laughing out loud again like old times.

I was excited to speak to Porsche and hear her side of the story. In our group, she was by far the loudest of all, so to hear her voice, strained like she'd come back from a war, hurt my heart. She told me about the scar going from her belly button on down and additional complications this would entail. Until then, I'd had nothing against Jerome, but now I hated him. She would never be the same. He had extinguished some of her light, and it was all his fault - all over a dumb argument.

Porsche told me how she felt during the time she was in a coma. To her, she was simply napping, but she understood it would be awhile before she'd wake up. She made plans in her head about all the things she had to do once she awakened again. The possibility of death never crossed her mind; she completely forgot human beings could die right until the point when she opened her eyes again. The first thing she saw was Jerome, who rushed out of his chair to grab her hand. He was about to apologize, but she cut him off and told him not to worry about it. Diamond even told me this incident brought the two of them closer. Porsche was seventeen, yet her level of strength and maturity was that of an older woman. Fully astonished and amazed by what she had done, I thought, *Who am I to be angry with him when Porsche herself has forgiven him?* and just like that, my anger towards him extinguished.

I walked away happy and uplifted by that phone call. That happiness disintegrated when I stopped by a council office and was told I didn't have the documents to ask for Mom and Dad's marriage certificate. That night I tossed and turned in the bed. That I was a homeless person with a job was something I was not ready to accept. Granted, the series of events that had led me here were not my fault, but the time for excuses was over. Sleep was not going to come, so I turned the lights on and stared at the list of items necessary for my new passport. *Every time I try to get a document, the road leads back to Mom and Dad and that stupid marriage certificate. What if I take Mom and Dad out of the equation?* I prayed for a few minutes and felt confident and reassured. I had a plan, and I would do whatever it took to get my passport.

The next day I packed my bookbag and travelled to the council in the arrondissement where I was born. Impressed by how large the building was, I headed straight to the passport service, a small office of about eight people. “Hi, I’m looking to have my passport renewed urgently; I have my old National Identification Card, passport photos and—”

“Here is a list of documents you will need, because this ID is way too old; how do I even know you’re French?” She slid the document over to me along with my ID and photos, then tilted her head to signal for the next customer. I moved, looking at her in the eyes.

“I lived in the US for eleven years, and my house burned down so I’ve come back; I don’t have these documents.”

“You need to at least have a family book.” “It was lost in the fire.”

“Ask your parents to—”

“They both perished in the fire,” I quickly replied. She took a deep sigh as her face went red.

“I do not understand where you came from. You don’t have half of the documents on this list, except an ancient ID, which for all I know you could have gotten from the streets! How do I know you’re French?!” she yelled.

I grabbed my ID and photos and stormed out of the room. Since this was the arrondissement I was born in, I went to the office down the hallway and asked for my birth certificate to be printed and stamped. Losing patience myself, I yanked the document out of the hands of the man who stamped it and marched right back to the passport service.

"There!" I slammed the birth certificate on her desk, startling her. "You feel that? It's still warm from the printer. I AM FRENCH!" She could hear the anger and pain. The entire office got quiet and looked at us. Shaking and at the brink of tears, I gave it one last shot. "Please, renew my passport."

She looked up at me then at the two security guards at the front door.

"*C'est bon.* She's clearly French," the colleague behind her casually said. She signaled for the security to stand down and picked up the birth certificate.

"Looks like you were born right here in the fourteenth arrondissement. Fine, give me what you've got, and let's get you a passport."

A few forms and 95 euros later, I was given the official receipt stating that the government was creating my passport. I walked out of the office feeling like I was on top of the world; in three days I would have a passport in my hands! Filled with excitement, I immediately hopped on a train to Disney's housing office.

"Et voilà!" The man at the counter said as he grabbed the receipt and typed in his computer. "We can do the paperwork on Monday," he said as he looked up at me and smiled.

"Sir, can this be done today instead?" I asked. He looked

at his watch.

"I've been sleeping out in the streets and have nowhere to go this weekend." He looked up at me with sympathy, then nodded and stood up. We went over to the apartment building, where I filled out the paperwork and signed on the many dotted lines. He then took me upstairs to my apartment. "Sorry, kid, this is the best I can do on such brief notice," he declared as he opened the door. I walked into a small hallway leading to the bathroom, then looked at the tiny corner kitchen and then the living space, which consisted of a table and sofa bed with an enormous window overlooking a roundabout leading to Disney.

"It's perfect!" I was so happy I hugged him, took the key, and caught the train back to Saint Dennis to get the rest of my things from the hostel. I opened the door to my new place in disbelief – the nightmare was over. I exhaled as though I had been holding my breath since the day I was told I would have to go to France and with this, the weight I had been carrying on my shoulders vanished.

As I got in the shower that night, I suddenly felt nauseous, something was making its way from my stomach, back up to my mouth like an erupting volcano. I swiftly leaned forward to limit the amount of vomit that would go all over me, instead, I burst into tears. Sobbing like I had never sobbed before. While wiping my tears, I noticed the water leaving my body was dark black; it had been a while since I could clean myself correctly. *This was hard, but you made it Sev, you made it. You're stronger than you think. Your determination and faith did this.* To my surprise when drying off, I had become two shades lighter. The black cloud which once hung over me this entire journey was finally gone.

As soon as I received the email stating my passport was ready, I went back to Paris to pick it up, then went over to see the Abdoula family. Mohamed kissed my passport when he saw it. "Now your new life begins, my child," he said while handing it back. I took the luggage I had left at their house over to my new apartment to unpack. I now had an actual address and a passport like everyone else. I looked up and whispered, *thank you, Jesus, for staying with me throughout this arduous time.*

30

JUST LIKE OLD TIMES

After staying in Haiti for some time with her siblings, Mom eventually bought a one-way ticket back to France. The house was occupied still, so she made arrangements to stay where I was originally meant to be; with Clarel, the family friend. A day after she landed, she wanted to see me. The timing couldn't have been better because I had just gotten my new place. We met outside of the Val D'Europe train station and walked to my studio.

"Welcome to my humble abode," I said as I opened the door and let her walk in first. She looked around for a moment and sat on the bed.

"It's not much, I know, but it's mine. For now, thanks to Disney," I declared while sitting on the chair across her.

"Bravo, you've done very well. Your father and I did not plan this for you, but you made it, and created your own little life here in France," she said.

We caught up a little about life since that Sunday brunch. It turns out, she only stayed a few days with Oncle Roness then stayed with Tante Judith who has a small mansion in

Haiti. Tante Judith gave Mom an entire floor to herself.

I vaguely told her about what I had gone through, leaving out major details. This chapter was behind me, and I had no desire to revisit it.

Carlene had heard that mom was coming to France and reached out to her and they began hanging out from time to time. Because of the things that I had told mom, she knew it was pointless to even ask me if I wanted to join them.

Things with Mom and I were good, until one day we were walking through the mall near the studio when my friend, Jacques, called me.

"Hey, just letting you know we are already at the movies, you on the way?"

Oh, Crap, I forgot we were doing movie night with the colleagues tonight!

"Uh, yeah, give me like fifteen minutes, I'm one station away. See you soon." I replied as I hung up. "Hey Mom, I'll have to leave, I'm meeting some of my friends for a movie."

"At this time?" she asked looking at her watch.

"It's eight o'clock," I replied defensively. "Let's walk to the station. Text me when you get home."

"I can see you're still behaving like a little *shit*," she said as her heels clicked louder and faster onto the pavement. My heart skipped a beat. This was the first time I ever heard Mom curse.

"It's just like you to do this, you know." She kept on walking, but I paused for a moment.

It dawned on me that Sunday brunch was only a few weeks ago. And despite everything she had gone through, very little to nothing had changed. Things were going to go right back to as though the knife incident had never occurred. *She's back to her old ways.*

Our relationship only went downhill from there. She made it a habit to call me and tell me about the awful things Carlene would say about me, how I stayed out late when I lived with her and I caused her to be at odds with her friend Josie. With each conversation, weight on my shoulders was coming back and growing heavier by the day.

I could only bear so much until the last straw came when she called and said that Carlene had spotted me smoking at work.

"Really, Mom?" I asked sarcastically

"How could you pick up such a nasty habit! This is not how I raised you."

"How could you think I would *ever* smoke? I've always told you I thought they cost too much health wise, I thought you knew your own daughter better," I answered, then made a lame excuse to get off the phone. *This ends now, I've gone through too much to go back to this.*

I needed to put some distance between us so Mom could no longer talk about me.

This was done subtly, a missed call here and there. Shorter Conversations that are fewer and further between, until I completely stopped answering all calls. Mom had made attempts to come by my apartment, but I was rarely ever home anymore since I hung out with colleagues more often. She had even stopped by my job once, but I sent her away. Finally, she gave up and I was glad; I needed that space for a while. My shoulders were light again, I was content without the slightest clue that years would pass before we would repair the relationship.

31

AN AMERICAN NIGHTMARE

Now that Mom and I were both out of the states, it was just Bridget and Dad in the house. For Dad, having to work to make the house payments and taking care of Bridget on his own was already stressful. Things didn't help when he became ill. This illness would differ greatly from anything he'd ever had; This time it was cancer. Although devastated because he wasn't able to take many sick days and we come from a family where words like 'unemployment' or 'sick leave' don't exist, he kept ongoing about his business. Over time, the diseases spread, making Dad lose weight rapidly, aging him, and making him weaker with each passing day.

The alarm rings. A ring so loud so sharp it could make your ears bleed. Dad turns over in his bed and reaches over to the alarm clock, giving it a weak tap, just barely turning it off. He slowly sits up on the side of the bed and prepares to stand up; putting his arms on either side of him but as he lifts himself up, he drops back into a sitting position. His arms are too weak to hold him. He takes a deep breath and tries again, using all his strength this time and successfully gets up. Slowly he puts one foot in front of the other, concentrating on staying up. Something caught in his throat quickly puts him in a coughing fit. He coughs so hard it knocks him off his balance and onto the floor. Down on his knees, Dad puts one hand to his mouth as he coughs, only to look back and see blood on it. He wipes his hand on his pajamas and gets back up and heads to the bathroom.

"Are you ok?" Bridget asked. "I came over because I heard you coughing."

"I'm fine," he responded quickly glancing at her before looking to the bathroom again. It was important not to show the pain walking was putting him in; he did not want to upset her.

"Are you going to work today?" she asked.

"Yes."

Only a few more steps, he thought, I'm almost there. He stops to lean on the wall, catching his breath from the walk. He coughs again; although he put his hand over his mouth, blood splattered on the white wall, on both the carpet and the tile. Dad briefly looks at Bridget, hoping she didn't see but it was too late. Bridget runs over to him, puts her hand on his shoulder and looks him in the eye.

"Dad, you're sick, you can't go to work like this," she pleaded.

"We need the money, we have to eat and pay for the house," he argued.

He turned his body away from her and took his first step away onto the bathroom tile. Underestimating how cold the tile was, and how fragile cancer made him, he screamed in agony at first contact; The tile under his foot felt like he just stepped onto a knife.

"Dad!" Bridget screamed, trying to pull him away from the tile.

"I'm fine Bridget, you can let go of me." He pulled his arm away. Bridget let him go and watched. He came over to the sink and splashed water on his face. She heard him coughing while walking away and poked her head in, checking to see if he was okay. There, she found him on the floor; his white pajamas, the bathroom cupboard, and all around him smothered in blood. With one hand on the counter, Dad tried to pull himself up, but he kept slipping on the blood. Saddened and fearful, Bridget felt the tears hitting her upper lip. She went over to him, stepping on the blood.

"Dad please, please stay home today. We'll figure something out for the bills just stay home and get some rest, you're not well," she pleaded.

He didn't answer nor show any sign that he even heard her, he just kept trying to get himself up off the floor and slipping every time. Realizing that there was nothing she could do, she retreated to the corner of the bathroom where she sat against the wall sobbing at the sight.

Bridget opened her eyes, luckily, it was all a dream, she sat up and looked around the room, then hugged her pillow, crying into it. She cried quietly, so she wouldn't wake Dad. She knew that although this was a dream, it was very close to reality as this was their lives now, this was what the cancer had done. It broke my heart when she told me about this dream, because I could only imagine what that must be like and considered myself lucky I did not have to witness this. Still, it was unfair for a nineteen-year-old kid to have to take on such responsibility; to have to live through this.

Dad, being as stubborn and proud as he was, didn't want to let something like cancer stop him from going to work. He missed days but kept trying to go to work as often as his deteriorating health would let him. When I spoke with Bridget, she would always mention how very strapped for cash they were and how hard things were for them. I knew that she was getting some money from Mom. But I also tried to top it up by sending them some money too. Dad was missing a few days of work here and there which soon became weeks.

We were never close, Dad and I. From the beginning he put a wall between the two of us, causing me to wonder sometimes if he even wanted to have kids or if Mom forced him into it. Over the years, our conversations became shorter and shorter. The few times he wasn't criticizing me or my friends, he would ask me if I needed money. I knew he had cancer, and that times were hard for Bridget and yet, it was hard for me to pick up the phone and call him. I felt guilty for being so far away and helpless, but was too hard headed to call him more often. After what I had gone through, I was selfish with my time and preferred to only have good vibes around me. When Bridget went off to college, I called him even less, partially because I didn't have to anymore but also because if I didn't, I wouldn't have to face the reality of things.

I had just turned 24, and this meant that the

government's financial generosity was growing thin. In France you get what we call APL. This is an effort to get young adults out of the house and into their first apartment, the government helps pay a part of the rent depending on your age and current employment. The amount of money gets smaller and smaller until it completely stops once you turn 26. As someone who was only 2 years away from no longer receiving any more help, this was not the best of financial times. I changed jobs from Disney to the Radisson hotel because they paid an extra 200 Euros.

I had just left the apartment I got from Disney, which had the rent at only 123 Euros a month and moved into a real place where the rent was 460 Euros a month not including bills such as light, electricity, property tax, and so on. I had taken a credit to make the initial deposit, and another one to buy myself furniture. Before I knew it that money was spent. The first of the month hit me like a ton of bricks when I received notice that all of my re-payments were due. I tried my best to make regular payments over to the US but was running low on money myself.

Only a day had passed after payday and the repayment yet when I checked my bank account there was only 30 euros left. I went to my calendar to see how many days left until my next paycheck and got fearful and looked around at the new apartment waiting for Mom and Dad to somehow appear out of thin air and help me; of course, that wasn't going to happen. Mom and I hadn't spoken in almost a year and Dad was over in the US. All I could do was cry. "What do I do now?" I asked myself. I needed to stay afloat to keep sending Bridget and Dad some money, even if it wasn't much, every little helped.

That night I didn't sleep; instead I stayed up to trying to come up with a plan. Sat on couch with the TV on starting into nothingness, I heard it, the magic word that changed everything: "Travailler plus pour gagner plus, work more to earn more." This was one of President Sarkozy's motto for making more money in France. This meant you could now work over the allotted 35hrs. I paid no attention to any of the terms and conditions of this and focused on the headline. "That's it!" I screamed out loud "I'll just do this the American way, I'll just work overtime!" I slapped my hands together and got on my computer. My resume was sent everywhere. There was no way you could have been in France for more than a week and not know that Severine Desrosiers was looking for a part-time job.

A few days later, I got a phone call from a hotel looking for a night auditor. I had loads of experience in hospitality and the interview went really well. They hired me on the spot and had me start the next evening. The night shifts are different, they expect you to check the work of the reception and restaurant for the day and make sure it financially makes sense. At first doing the 'financial closure' as they called it took every minute of the night but once I figured out the system and added a couple of formulas in the spreadsheet, I could do the reconciliation in one hour; leaving me the rest of the night to sleep in a rollaway bed I found in the downstairs office.

I had this routine down to a tee which quickly built up my reputation. Management started talking about me and it didn't take long before they offered me another job at their sister hotel during the weekends. Weekends were my days off as I was already working full time at the Marriott hotel and doing a couple of nights at the KUBE but because I was living off of rice and pasta, I took the job. The brilliant thing about working in hotels is that the food is taken care of.

The first of the month came around again and so did the paychecks. The two additional paychecks plus the very generous client tips allowed me to send money to Bridget again. Financial victory came at a price. I was getting tired, and the few times I got some time off, I'd be too tired to do the groceries and when I had the energy, I was like a zombie. I wanted to cut back on the hours, but Bridget and Dad were still very broke and with Bridget in college over in North Carolina, the travel back and forth to Georgia became expensive. With his health degrading, Dad could only work so many days if at all. On top of this, my own loans were still here.

Exhausted, instead of cutting back on the hours, I asked the manager to schedule me in as much as possible. He gave me a blank calendar for the month and said:

"You're one of the best auditors that we have, just tell me which days you can come in and I'll make sure you work those shifts."

I practically filled out every day, giving myself a 4 day off for the month. My number one goal was to stay afloat and keep sending money to the US. They needed it and so did I. My schedule was crazy: I started work at the Murano at 11pm and would finish at 7am, then I'd hop into a taxi and start a 7am shift and finish at 3pm, but most of the time I would finish later. There I would find another hotel nearby if I was too tired to go home to sleep until 8ish and would get ready for my 10pm shift at the KUBE. The rotation would go on like this for a few weeks. There was even a time when I left my house on Thursday morning and didn't come back until Sunday night because I was working back to back.

Everyone saw I was not the same; I looked exhausted. I was like a machine; I kept going. I had noticed my thinking had slowed down and I would make rookie errors. But the motivation to hurry and make this money to send over to the states kept me going. The few colleagues that knew about my situation asked if I was taking drugs to keep up. Honestly, I wasn't even sure how I kept up either. My exhaustion only grew worse, I started micro sleeping; at one point and time I even slept standing up, mid-sentence it was insane. Soon I started missing entire shifts completely but Katie, who left the millennium hotel to work at Marriott with me would cover for me. Had it been up to me, I would have just kept going but one day, while on my way to work, I noticed I couldn't put my foot into my ballerina correctly; when I looked down, I realized it was because my foot had swollen twice its size.

After a couple of attempts to get my foot in my shoe, I called in sick at work, then made a doctor's appointment which I slept through so had to call in sick the next day and booked the earliest appointment to make sure I didn't fall asleep. I was on bedrest for 2 weeks and although I desperately needed it, I worried about Dad and Bridget. In between that time, I managed to land myself another job but this time in an office which paid me a couple of hundred more than the Marriott hotel did.

The money I was sending was like a drop in the ocean because mortgage payments were being missed. As much as he tried, Dad wasn't able to make them anymore. One day, the official letter for foreclosure came. Dad's English was at a beginner's level at best but it was as though a universal language was used to draft this. The inevitable reared its ugly head and Bridget told me about the last days.

She told me about how she walked in the sitting room one day which only had chairs since he had since sold the table. She saw him sitting and looking around and with a single look at Dad she knew. No need to talk. Taking a seat across from him, they both sat in silence, staring out into nothingness.

A house once filled with laughter and hopes of the

American dream was now a nightmare and a heavy burden. Everything Mom and Dad had worked for had fallen apart piece by piece and this was the last domino. Mom and I were in France now and Bridget was going back and forth from Charlotte, North Carolina to Georgia so it's not like we needed the house now anyway.

They sat there in silence for hours. Who knew they would be the last two standing in this house when we bought it? Back to square one, over to Will's house was the only option. Beatrice made it known she was unhappy about the situation and told Dad many times that she couldn't wait for him to die. Relieved Bridget could get herself an apartment close to school, he put his pride aside, and moved back to his brother's house, into the basement; just like the beginning.

32

RACE AGAINST TIME

I gave Dad a quick call as it had been a really long time since I had called him and not Bridget. Wishing he wouldn't pick up, it stopped ringing after the first ring.

"Allo."

"Papa?"

"Ah Severine, wow long time."

"Yes it has been, how are you?"

"I'm perfectly fine. Oh, I saw your friend the other day, Porsche was it? She looks like a complete bum now, you sure know how to pick your friends."

"Oh, it must have been a grim day for her, I guess. How's your health? Are the meds—"

"I said I was fine!" he yelled. Afraid he would go on a tantrum, I took his word for it.

"Okay that's good- listen I've got to go. I'll speak to you later."

Ease came over me as I hung up. I called Bridget a day after, who told me about the house. It pained me to hear but thought there was no need for 2 people to live in a 5 bedroom house. I had missed her a lot and wanted to see her again, so I offered for us to go on a holiday, just the two of us but she turned me down.

The swelling in my leg had gone down dramatically, but it was now permanently deformed forcing me to slow the night shifts to a crawl.

I had always known I would not be able to keep up such a pace. Lucky for me, a recruitment company called to tell me about a new company, Regime Coach, looking for an Administrator in central Paris, and after
2 interviews I landed the role. Regime coach was a small dieting company which started when Dr. Dukan helped his secretary lose 50kg over the course of a year; Momentum continued when rumors about a member of the royal family successfully losing weight while on this diet swirled around. Dr. Dukan struck while the iron was hot and created Regime Coach which then expanded to all of Europe, the US, and Australia. Everyone at Regime Coach was relatively new and learning along the way like any other startup.

The same month I stopped this, was the same month my bank account harshly reminded me that my repayments were still due. I tried to call one hotel during my break and in the meantime prepared to live on 100 euros for the month.

One day while at work, I saw a text from my cousin Patrice.

Patrice was around 5yrs older than me. He and I grew up together in France and then one day his parents dropped him off at Beatrice's house because they wanted to retire to Haiti. He first lived with us for a couple of months and then went right back to Beatrice's house where he befriended Willson, Farah, and their cousin. During their teenage years and even some adult years, Patrice followed Willson through his partying ways. This eventually got him in so much trouble that Beatrice kicked him out and he went back to France.

Because of my fond memories of the times we would play with dolls and how nice he has always been with me; he was my favorite cousin. When I learned that he went back to France, it took us a full year to finally sync our schedules to see each other. We loved each other but from afar, therefore I thought it was weird he would text out of the blue so I stepped out of the office and called him.

"Hey Patrice what's up."

"Oh hey cuz." For the first time he sounded serious. "Everyone is saying that your Dad is sick, are you OK?"

"Yeah, I know he has cancer, but he told me himself he was fine."

"No cuz, he's not; it's really bad, I heard they moved him to a hospice."

"Oh my god! I've got to go."

I went straight to my managers Monique and Jarvis' office. Monique had gone home so I told Jarvis what was going on. He hugged for about five minutes and told me to go and see Dad and come back when I'm ready. I was outside waiting for my temporary roommate Silvia to come pick me up when it dawned on me. *How the hell am I supposed to pay for a flight?* Suddenly, I got the idea to call Katie. Since we met at the Millennium a couple of years ago, Katie, her boyfriend, and I had become close. She was the kind of friend I did not need to call daily but would do any and everything for should she need. I called her and told her about it. I was ashamed to even tell her what was happening before I got the chance to officially ask her if I could borrow money. She just said, "Leave it with me," and hung up the phone. The next day early morning I received a call from Antoine.

"Hi Antoine, you ok?"

"Hey, I'm good. Listen, grab a pen and paper." Asking no questions I did as instructed and wrote what he told me to.

"This the number to my Amex card; take whatever you need and pay us back whenever you can."

"Oh my gosh thank you both so, so much," I said teary eyed.

"You're welcome Sev, now go see your Dad."

I immediately went to my laptop and searched for flights and the earliest and cheapest flight I could find was doing a layover in Germany. Like a mad woman, I rushed to my closet and dumped any and everything that would fit in a suitcase even though I was only doing 5 days in the

US. Sylvia treated me to our favorite buffet restaurant in Meaux then took the bus to the airport.

"Here," she opened my hand and gave me a wad of cash. "I wanted to thank you for all that you've done for me and I know this isn't much but I know it will help you."

"Thanks," I answered while giving her a hug.

Minutes after reaching the airport, a call from an unknown number comes through. I just looked at the phone ringing and kept walking to the check-in desk. I went up to the delta check-in desk and the lady was having trouble finding my reservation. The number kept ringing and since there was no one behind me in the line, I picked it up.

"Hello?"

"Hi, I am calling from Expedia. I understand you booked the flight to go to the US?"

"Yes I did."

"Okay, I'm sorry to inform you your flight isn't valid because the credit card isn't the same name as the passenger. We would need for you to send the ID of the cardholder."

"And you tell me this now?! Why did you allow me to book the flight though? How come you didn't tell me this prior?! I'm literally standing at the check-in desk, standing before one of your colleagues!"

"Oh, you were supposed to send the ID card for that person."

"Well, can I try to do this now?"

"No, no, you're supposed to do this earlier. We couldn't

contact you earlier to tell you because our offices were closed."

"Ma'am, I'm trying to hurry and go to the states to see my Dad who's dying of cancer. I'm sorry he couldn't die during your operating hours; let me call him and ask that he reschedules his death to fit in your schedule better."

She could hear the pain and frustration in my voice, so she placed me on hold for a few minutes and told me it was all okay. It relieved me; I honestly wasn't sure if Antoine could even send me his ID on time before my flight. Sylvia gave me a hug, and I went through security. It wasn't until I was in the queue to hand my passport over and board my flight that I remembered this flight was going to Germany first. *I don't have a place to stay!* Lucky for me, I remembered I still had my Marriott employee card I had 'forgotten' to hand back when I handed in my resignation. The card allowed me to stay in any Marriott hotel at a discounted rate. I quickly looked for the Marriott closest to the airport and booked it for the night. The flight to Germany was quick; I got out and immediately looked for a taxi. The man didn't speak any English, so I showed him my phone and said:

"Frankfurt Marriott hotel." He nodded and started the car. While on the road, I booked my other hotel stay in Georgia; I wasn't sure where I would stay because I didn't tell anyone I was coming and thought it was a safe bet to play with customs once at the airport. Even though I had a good discount, staying at the hotel would take up almost all of my money so I would have to be cautious out there. Preoccupied, I hadn't noticed we had been driving for over half an hour. I panicked for 2 minutes but calmed down when I saw the Marriott sign.

"Hi, I've got a reservation for the night under Ms. Desrosiers." The receptionist smiled and typed my name in the computer. Two minutes passed by before I showed her the same screen I showed the taxi driver.

"Oooooh," she says as she grabs my phone "Okay this is Frankfurt Marriott hotel but you are booked at Frankfurt Airport Marriott hotel," She then picked up a city map and opened it up.

"The hotel is waaaaaaay down here. Should I call another taxi?" I had already spent a lot on the first one.

"No need, can I get there by public transport?"

"Yes but you must hurry, everything will close soon," she answered and wrote on the map with a pen. The markings went on for a few minutes, making me think twice about that taxi. This trip would take me on the other side of town. She then explained it to me and it didn't seem so bad; at least not until I walked out of the hotel in the dark, with the snow, and no sign of Wi-Fi. *You have to get to the other side of town; you can do this Sev.* To save time just in case I missed a connection, I started with a slow jog in the mall and just followed the signs to the train like she told me. At one point and time I was standing on a small train platform outside in the dark. All you could see was snow and thanks to the Wi-Fi no longer available on my phone I didn't know if the train was coming in one minute or two hours.

All I can do is pray to God this is the right train for the right direction. I looked at the map a thousand times while waiting for the train. Finally, the train came; unable to pronounce any of the stations, I listened attentively for every station, and would check it off on the map until it was time to change platforms again. Finally, according to the list I was waiting on my last train which also happened to the very last train for the night so no room for errors. After following the receptionist's directions meticulously, I made it to the Frankfurt Airport Marriott Hotel.

The receptionist quickly checked me in, and I crashed on the bed, getting only 3 hours of sleep because. *Next is the US.* In the middle of the night I frantically called Lamar and asked him to draft a letter saying how long I have worked with them and the date at which I intended to come back so I could give it to immigration if need be. Without asking any questions, he sends this over to me signed later that hour.

The next day I get to the airport after a 6 minute drive. As soon as we boarded the plane, my stomach started hurting and all the painful memories came rushing back during the flight.

But as we started getting closer and closer to the States, my stomach started to hurt. *What if they turn me away? What would I tell Sylvia and all my friends? would I be able to see my Dad at all?* My mind was racing the entire way.

The customs line came, and I thought I would poop my pants. I stood in front of an officer who smiled while taking my passport. He switched his glance back and forth between my face and my passport. Finally came what I feared most out of his mouth:

"Come with me please." There we were, walking into a room in the back. He hands me over to another officer who nicely asks me why I'm here. I gave him my passport, the letter Lamar had sent me and the hotel reservation I had booked and told him that Dad was in a hospice. He went into another room while I closed my eyes and prayed. He came back telling me that my story checked out so they would let me go through.

I stepped out of the airport and was excited to see Diamond and Bridget again. I got into a taxi en route to the Marriott.

"What brings you to Georgia?" he asked.

"I'm here to see my Dad, he's dying of cancer."

"Sorry to hear that." I smiled and thanked him. I got my phone out and called Diamond, both she and Bridget happened to be together.

"Guys I'm on my way!!! Whoooooooooohoooooo!" We all started screaming and laughing on the phone. Confused, the taxi driver asked again slowly to make sure he understood what I said.

"So, your Dad is dying?"

"Yeah." I knew what my excited screaming looked like

but didn't feel like explaining myself to him. When I got to the hotel, I flashed my Marriott employee card to the receptionist who proceeded with the discounted rate but in the middle of the check-in I saw Diamond and Bridget. I dropped everything and ran to them well all screamed, laughed, and cried as we hugged the life out of each other for about 10min.

The receptionist got teary eyed herself looking at the reunion.

"What are you doing here?" Diamond asked. "Just stay over at my house."

I apologized to the receptionist, and we were on our way.

"Hey Sevie, you got a little wider huh?" Diamond's Mom said as she hugged me. I stepped into the house and saw Jerome at the top of the stairs smoking.

"Hey Sevie, long time," he said.

I paused for a moment. *Who are you to stay mad when Porsche didn't?*

"Hi, how are you?" I replied.

We ate and laughed for hours. Unsure if it was the wine or my jet lag starting to hit me but I felt dizzy so went to their living room downstairs next to Diamond's room where Bridget and Diamond slept. Two hours later I felt someone hug me; I looked, and it was Porsche.

She was thin but still exquisite. "Oh my God! You're here!" she screamed with wide eyes. We hugged for a while and even exhausted, I stayed up for a couple more hours just to chat with her. The next day, Diamond drove me to Willson and Farah's house who I called earlier to let them know I was here. I walked into the house and was greeted by the entire family who all hugged me and were happy to see me. As soon as they left the room, Beatrice offered me a drink of water and sat next to me.

"Hey sweetie you ok? How are you?" I knew this was just to get the formalities out of the way.

"I'm fine, I'm just staying for a couple of days if that's ok."

"Yes, yes that's fine. Bridget is here too?" Bridget had not bothered going through the primary entrance, instead she went through the side door which used to lead to our old apartment but was now Willson's bachelor pad. As soon as I nodded yes, Beatrice's face changed like that of Jekyll and Hyde.

"When this is over, I don't want Bridget to set foot in my house ever again." Taken back I wanted to ask why but knew it was a terrible idea.

"She's been nothing but disrespectful and rude to me." I stopped listening after that. I knew my sister and knew how Beatrice operated. *Is she serious right now? Does she really think it's appropriate to talk about this now?* I thought. Furious, I tried to think about something else as she was rambling on and on. Now and then I would throw in a "uh-huh," or "that's crazy," to seem interested. I vowed to myself never to go back to her house once this was over either.

Later that day, Will drove Bridget and I to see Dad at the hospice while on his way to drop Beatrice off at work. "Haven't you gone to the hospice enough? He's dying, you need to let him go and be with your family. You were his personal driver taking him to and from the doctor's appointments, wasting our gas, and now this? What about your wife and kids huh?" Beatrice was on a rant again. Bridget and I sat in the back listening to her complaining right up until she got dropped off to work.

"I'm coming back in a bit," Will said as he dropped us off. With one hand I could count the amount of times I had been in a hospital even though both Mom and Dad worked at WellStar in Cobb County at one point and time. Hospitals to me were a sad place but hospices were much different. While I'm not sure what other hospices look like, this one just looked like an old folks' home. Very welcoming with dated furniture and decor.

The nurse at reception took me to Dad's room where a ghost of Dad's self lay before me. Years of eating rice had given him what I called a 'rice gut' . It looked very similar to a beer gut but was usually smaller. All the Haitian Dads had one and Dad was no exception. The cancer made him lose so much weight that his stomach sunk inwards instead, leaving him a frail looking man. He always had a twinkle in his eyes, we all did; slanted eyes with a twinkle must have been a dominant gene because all of his children, Carlene, Delphine, Bridget, and I had it but Dad had lost his. His eyes were glazed over. He looked like he had aged 20yrs. Had the nurses not walked us to his room, I probably would have passed him right by without knowing it.

"Papa?" He slowly turned his head, glimpsed me and turned back.

"You look so different Dad, like you're in pain." He showed no signs of responsiveness.

"Bridget and I, we can take care of ourselves now, don't feel you have to hold on for us. We will eventually be okay. You don't have to endure this because of us. You can let go."

He didn't speak, but was drooling so Bridget went to the bathroom to grab some tissue to clean him up. Bridget told me that even though he was in a hospice, she was happy that he wasn't over at Beatrice's house. The illness would cause him to throw up, and sometimes even soil himself and with Mom and I gone and Bridget off to college, there were many times when Beatrice and Will were left to clean up after him.

When she could, Bridget would spend the weekend over at their house to be with Dad and Beatrice would make her feel guilty for even going to school instead of taking care of her father. Knowing that Bridget was there, Beatrice sometimes would lock Bridget and Dad in the basement when she went off to work, knowing there was nothing to eat in the fridge. She would constantly tell Dad how she couldn't wait until he died because he was such a burden.

My heart broke listening to this, and I wondered, how was Bridget able to deal with all of this? But then again, it's not like she had a choice, all Mom and I could do was just send money when we could; or at least I assumed Mom was sending money, I was still not speaking to her so didn't know for sure. We stayed with Dad for another hour before going back to Will's house.

Willson was home and invited us to his side of the house and once she finished work, Diamond joined us. Not much had changed, Willson would get together with the same crowd of friends he has had since our high school days and they would drink and hang out. The more people started trickling in at his place, the more drinks he would have. He got so wasted that at one point and time, he turned to me and said:

"Check this out check this out! I woke up today, go to work, live my life, and next thing I know my cousin Severine is here. I can't believe it man, that's what's up!" Diamond and I looked at each other and laughed. I loved the fact that Willson was a funny drunk. Aside from the time he completely flipped over a drunk guy accidently spilling his drink on my shoe at a party and he stopped the music and turned the lights back on to curse him out, drinking would usually bring out his funny, mellowed-out side of him.

"Cuz, you're more than welcome to just stay here. Instead of being in the house with everyone else. You can just hang out," he said, handing me an extra key.

"Thanks, I'll take you up on that offer."

I spent the next day hanging out with Bridget in the house's basement. We watched a couple of seasons of *True Blood* together and caught up. Diamond then called me and wanted to hang out just the two of us. I checked with Bridget that it was OK and she just nodded her head.

"Come back here tonight though, I don't want to sleep in the room Dad was staying in by myself, it's too weird."

"Okay, I'll come back later then."

Diamond and I went to go see her best male friend, Daniel, and his roommate. We hung out, drank, and ate together. We played a drinking game which I kept losing causing me to toss back the vodka shots back to back. Diamond went home and left me with the boys, it was still early so we kept drinking and talking. The time flew by and I finally asked Daniel to take me home but he asked me to wait a little since he had had a few drinks himself. Sat on the couch, I told myself I would rest my eyes for a moment until he was sober enough to take me home. When I opened my eyes, I had 3 missed calls from Bridget and it was 6am. I panicked and brutally shook Daniel awake, who hopped in the car with one eye open.

"I told you to take me home! My sister will be pissed," I told him.

"I'm so sorry I fell asleep, here let me take you to McDonald's first to get her some breakfast," he replied.

I ran back to the house and tried to enter quietly hoping

that she wouldn't have noticed the time it was, but she was awake already.

"Here I bought you some food. I'm so sorry about last night." I said, handing her over the McDonald's bag.

"Eat your food Severine," she replied while getting her bag ready. She was headed back to school.

"You ready?" Will asked. We drove to central Atlanta so she could take the bus back to North Carolina. On the way, we got a little lost, unsure of which station to go to so Will stopped the car and told us to ask for directions. Bridget immediately got out of the car and started walking. Surprised, Will looked at me and asked, "Aren't you going to get out of the car to help her?" It's not that I didn't want to, I could tell she didn't want me there. Naturally she was still mad, but I got out of the car and caught up with her. Back before I had left the states, I would have been the one to ask but things had changed, Bridget had been left here on her own for a couple of years now and she was no longer the little girl who hid behind her big sister. She was taking the lead on this and asking anyone she could find on the quiet streets of Atlanta for directions. I felt like an inconvenience; like an old suitcase that has lost a wheel and is a pain to drag along because it slows you down but I said nothing. Out of place, because I wasn't sure where in Atlanta we were, I let her do her thing and jogged after her as she quickly walked from one person to another until she was sure of which station we needed to go to. She eventually found the place, and we parted ways. We hugged, but it was not like before, it had nothing to do with the embrace she had given me when I first arrived. This was a one arm hug, forced because Will was standing there; necessary because we both weren't sure of when we would see each other again.

"Bye," she said as she turned and got on the bus, without looking back as Will and I hoped back into the car and quietly drove back to the house.

"Hey Cuz, what you trynna do today? You want to hang out or go somewhere?" Willson said as I entered his house.

"I think I just want to visit my Dad today if you don't mind?" I replied.

"No, I don't; I think it's a good idea, actually. I'll drop you off first, go to work and come back for you."

We got to the hospice and checked in with the nurse at reception.

"He's declining fast, it won't be long now. He keeps getting out of bed and tries to get out of the room like he's got somewhere he needs to go." The nurse said, while looking at Willson. They spoke amongst each other for a few minutes like I was invisible. I couldn't blame her. She had seen Willson a lot more than she had seen me. I made my way to his room.

"Hi Dad." He was unresponsive. A few seconds later, Willson walked into the room with a bright smile and enthusiasm.

"Hey Joseph, how are you?" he asked.

"Heeeyyy Willson." Dad's face lit up. "How are you?" They started speaking in Creole for a bit. Dad was happy, he was even making jokes and laughing, just having Willson in the room brought him back to his old self again and for a moment, it was like Dad almost forgot he was dying of cancer. Willson fed him a yoghurt at Dad's request but he was full after two spoonful's. Although I was unnoticed and stood in the corner of the room like a fly on the wall, their interaction was heart-warming.

"I've got to go to work now. Take it easy ok?" he said as he walked out. Dad's eyes followed Willson, and he quickly turned his head back and started at the wall in front of him. I wanted to take the opportunity to speak to him now that I knew he was responsive.

"Hey Dad, how are you?"

"Good."

"I see you've lost your rice gut. Now I'm the one with the gut," I laughed as I touched my stomach.

"On my way over I was contemplating getting you some perfume from Yves St Laurent but was advised against it." Dad chuckled.

I smiled, grabbed a chair to sit on and watch TV. We didn't say anything more, but I was happy to be spending time with him, even if it was in a hospice. For once, I was content hanging out with my Dad.

Throughout the day a couple of people came to visit; family, friends, co-workers that were all Haitian. The Haitian community was a large one and many of them knew Dad. This made me realize how little I knew of him because I had no idea he had that many friends. Oncle Evens who I hadn't seen since he told me I had to leave the country also passed by.

I stayed in the room watching TV until the door opened again.

"Bath time!" One nurse declared. "Sweetie, you must leave the room for this." As instructed, I stepped out of the room and went back to reception.

"Ouch! Ouch! It hurts." I had never heard Dad scream in pain before, let alone scream in English. Unable to bear it, I broke down in tears and sobbed for a few minutes. The nurse at reception handed me some tissue and smiled without saying a word. When I came back in the room, I could tell they had sedated him with something to ease the pain. He was muttering nonsense in creole for hours and looking at the wall when suddenly he became quiet. In a moment of complete clarity and self-awareness he turned to me and said:

"I'm going to go to sleep now." He stared at me.

"Okay Dad, goodnight," I answered. He turned his head back and closed his eyes while I watched TV until Willson came back. I told him about how he was screaming when the nurses gave him a bath.

"This happens a lot. I'm still traumatized from the night we drove him to the hospice, he was in such pain and there was nothing we could do you know?" Willson answered. We ate dinner and went straight to bed.

"Come on, we gotta go." Willson told me as he shuffled me back and forth so I would wake up. "They need to see you."

"For what?" I asked as I tried to open the other eye.

"They just need to see you. Get dressed," he replied.

We drove silently. It was too early to make conversation. I wondered what new information the nurses had that they couldn't tell me over the phone. As soon as I approached reception, the nurse got up to give me a hug.

"I'm sorry honey, he's passed."

It all made sense now, why Willson didn't want to say anything. I sat on a chair and cried, next to a lady that knew Dad from work. She was a complete stranger to me but she took me in her arms, regardless.

"There, there honey I know how you feel. Just last month, I lost my Dad," she said while caressing my head. I pulled my head off her chest to look at her.

"I'm sorry to hear that. I'm sorry you know how I feel," I replied while continuing to sob.

Willson sat by me uncomfortably. He didn't know what to say and I didn't expect him to say anything. What does one say in such situations, anyway? Guilt came pouring in about how I hadn't called enough, how I wasn't able to do much more than just send money when a voice came into my head. *You know why you're here. you've made it against all odds, and we both know God brought you here. He brought me here to say goodbye so let's just be thankful. Be thankful we got to say goodbye this time and hold on to that.* The tears stopped falling, and I was thankful instead; I got to be here and say goodbye in my own way.

I called Bridget who had already received a call from the nurses then called Diamond and told her the news. To my surprise, Porsche called me crying. Dad never liked either Diamond and Porsche because he thought they were a bad American influence on me but that didn't stop the both of them from caring about him; knowing this made me smile and appreciate the both of them even more.

The funeral wasn't going to happen until a week after but I was only staying 2 more days. Terrified to even attempt to change the flights, a part of me was relieved I couldn't come because I felt so out of place and like a burden to everyone now; I also wasn't sure I could handle his funeral. Since I barely made it out of the airport the first time around, I didn't want the American Immigration after me if I changed my flights. It was best for me to go on the original day I was meant to.

Not in the mood to stay in the house, I gave Jay a call. He had called me a few days back when he saw my status update on Facebook and took two days off to hang out with me. I booked a Marriott hotel in Atlanta for us to stay in. Although I was sad, I still was excited to see Jay again after so many years. We ate and drank that night while catching up on everything and the next day we went to the mall. The two days went by really quickly and we hugged for about 10min before leaving. I went back to the house and had one last dinner with Diamond and her boyfriend Jared and got to know him a little. He was a male masseuse who had met Diamond through Porsche, who used to work as the receptionist in the office. The next morning, Farah offered to take me to the airport. Her offer couldn't have come at a better time because I had asked Diamond who was too busy, and Willson had to go to work; I would have called myself a taxi but was unsure of whether I could even afford to pay them.

She gave me a long hug, and I got back on a plane to France. I had missed Bridget, Diamond, and Porsche a lot and was overall happy to have seen everyone again. Still, I was happy to be back home to be back in France. *Is this our relationship now?* I wondered as I looked back at the way Bridget and I had left things. *Will we be like these people that say they have a sibling in another city or country they barely speak to?* When I landed, I was happy because the US was no longer a place I could ever call home anymore.

33

COPING

I landed on a Tuesday night and was due back at work Wednesday morning. It felt good to be back, I had missed my routine and even being around my colleagues at Regime Coach. It turns out, I was the first person to have lost a family member while working there, so when management learned about my father dying, they scrambled to put a bereavement procedure together.

If you do what you used to do, you will eventually feel like you used to. I muttered this to myself over and over on my way to work on Wednesday morning, yet the closer I got to the front door of the office, the heavier my legs felt. Scared and anxious, I suddenly began having trouble breathing. I took one step inside the office and immediately felt the arms of all thirteen of my colleagues wrapping around me like a warm blanket on a cold winter day. Somehow they sensed I needed a hug right then and there. One of them handed me an envelope and a small black notebook before walking back to her desk. The envelope contained some money, which came just in time because I was super broke, and the notebook had hand-written messages and quotes from each of them about loss and dealing with grief. My breathing went back to normal; I was taken aback by their efforts and compassion.

As I was typing, a thought came into my head: *I no longer have a Dad whom I emotionally keep at arm's length; he is just gone.* Trying to remain calm, I rushed to the bathroom, locked myself in a stall, and sobbed my heart out. Only a few minutes had passed before I heard a knock on the door from Monique, one of my managers. I unlocked the bathroom stall and looked at her with red, puffy eyes.

"Oh, sweetie, are you okay? Is there anything I can help you with?" she asked.

Unable to utter anything just yet, I just shook my head no.

"Do you want to go home?" I shook my head again, my eyes burning as tears pierced through them. She looked concerned and helpless. Monique and I had a great work relationship; I had become her work daughter and could tell it was painful for her to see me this way.

"It's okay, Monique. There's nothing you can do right now. I think I just need to let it out. I'll take a couple more minutes and get back to work if that's all right," I finally answered.

"Okay, take all the time you need. I'm here if you need to talk," she responded and walked away.

I sat there a couple more minutes before going back to

my desk. Needless to say, I was upset about Dad's passing but was also disgusted with myself for letting Bridget down so badly. I kept trying to picture what life was like for her during this time – seeing Dad go from a healthy man to a walking corpse and managing life in the US while Mom and I were a whole continent away. How did she deal with all that? And had it been me, would I have dealt with it any better? I had so many questions and pondering about it only made me feel worse.

I didn't want to admit it out loud, but I was glad I was not there for the funeral. I wanted to be as far away as possible to avoid the pain of it all. I justified everything by saying it would have been too big a risk for me to take with immigration, considering everything that I had to go through just to see Dad in the first place. I dealt with Dad's death the same way I had dealt with Delphine's, by trying to get back to normal. I hung onto the fact that I got to say goodbye, which was a gift in itself.

I called Bridget the day of the funeral and sensed that we were still not okay. There was no need to continue with small talk – I wanted to lay the issue bare and attack the elephant in the room.

"What's wrong?" I asked.

"So you never kept in touch with me, and you weren't there for Dad and me," she said calmly.

"Well, I did call you as much as I—"

"But you weren't there! You didn't even come to the

funeral! I was alone," she interrupted. I could hear the pain in her voice.

"Bridget, I did the best I could. I had already booked the return flight."

"Diamond was more of a sister to me than you ever were!" she responded.

"That's not fair. Do you know the lengths I've gone through to make sure that you and I can talk on the phone like this? And when was the last time you ever called me? Ever? You take all this for granted, so the next time, why don't you call me instead?" I lashed back at her.

We hung up just like that. I was sobbing. *Did I mess up the bond she and I had?* But then a few days later, to my surprise, she called. Somehow she managed to buy a calling card. We both apologized over the phone. I cried then too. She could finally see things from my point of view, and I was over the moon, but mostly I was grateful she had forgiven me. I still kicked myself for not being there for her when she needed me the most.

A couple of months before, I had made plans to go to Marrakech for my birthday with three of my closest friends, whom I'd met back in my hotel days. Right after booking the trip, I was looking forward to it, but then Dad died, and I wanted to cancel it all.

But my friends convinced me not to. They told me that Dad would have wanted me to live my life to the fullest and that the trip would do me some good, and so we went, and for those three short days, I forgot about everything. I was living in the moment. Time flies when you're having fun, I guess, because I was on my way back home in the blink of an eye. Sylvia had moved out a couple of months back to live with her boyfriend, so I had my studio to myself again. I walked into the quiet studio and had to look around for a moment to make sure I was in the right place. *Was the studio always this large?*

There was barely any time to get settled back into work because I was off again two weeks later. I had taken two weeks off for the holidays with no clue what to do. The idea of cancelling them just seemed sad to me, but the thought had crossed my mind. On Christmas Day, a few friends sent me messages asking me to come over so I wouldn't spend Christmas alone. I politely declined and told them I had company. That was a lie – I was alone. I didn't have the strength to pretend to be happy, and I didn't want to bring everyone down with my sad mood.

I sat around the house alone until New Year's Eve, when Sarah, an old friend from my hotel days who had just moved to London invited me over for celebrations. Without thinking twice, I packed up a bag and went for a few days. London was a blast! It reminded me of a smaller version of the US. Everyone was so nice and polite – it was unreal, but just like Marrakech, I came back home to what looked like an even bigger and emptier space.

After looking at the pictures from Marrakech and New

Year's Eve in London, I decided to start working out and to concentrate on being healthy. Since I worked for a diet company, I figured I might as well put their method to use. Even though it was winter, I went out every morning and ran. The results didn't take long to follow, and for a while, this kept me occupied – until it didn't.

The studio was getting larger and emptier by the minute. When I was at work, I was sleepy from boredom, and when I was at home, I felt lonely. It was time to make a change. *London was really cool; maybe I should move there for a couple of months and see how it goes and after that, possibly Australia?* I entertained those thoughts for a month without acting on them.

Annoyed with myself, I marched into the office at Regime Coach the next morning and handed in my notice. Right after work, I handed in my notice at Orpi, my property rental agency.

Okay, Sev, you can stay here, become homeless and jobless in about a month, or you can start looking at how to move to London. It can't be that hard; Mom and Dad switched continents with three kids and no grip on the English language. You're bilingual with no kids; this is a piece of cake!

That weekend, I sought Mom out to make peace. A part of me was still angry about the way she yelled at me for hours for no reason, telling me about how I had ruined my life. It upset me even more when I saw that despite everything we had gone through, she and I, she still maintained the same toxic behavior when we saw each other again in France. I was angry, but too much time had passed, and now with Dad gone, it was just the three of us, so I had to make things right.

My last month went by quicker than I'd expected. I barely had any real time to organize my housing, yet the mere thought of moving excited me. I had called an old friend, Melanie, from my hotel days and told her I was coming to London, and she told me to stay with her until I found a place. I was so excited, I didn't even want to wait for my last paycheck to hit my account to book my bus ticket – for the first time in a long time, I had something to look forward to. Ill-prepared, with a little over £50 to my name and the promise I could stay at an old friend's place, I got on a bus to London and started my new chapter.

34

HOW PRECIOUS LIFE IS

I arrived in London with a large piece of luggage, a little over £50, and lots of enthusiasm. Melanie waited for me at the bus station.

"Had a good trip?" she asked.

"Yeah, it was cool," I answered.

"Listen, remember how I told you it was fine for you to crash at mine?" She smiled sheepishly.

Worried, I replied, "Yeah…"

"Well, my place isn't exactly finished yet, so we'll be crashing at my colleague's place. His name is George." She saw the look on my face and tried to reassure me. "Don't worry, he's cool. I already told him you were coming, and he's fine with it. Anyway, that cool with you?"

"Yes, I—"

"Great, because we're pretty much on the way to his house now," she exclaimed with a grin. We walked towards his house in what seemed like total darkness until a front porch light came on, grabbing our attention.

"That must be him," Melanie said as she walked faster.

Soon after, a short, thin man with olive skin and dark hair stepped outside to the front porch. He leaned against the door, readjusting himself every couple of seconds as we got closer.

"Hey, George!" Melanie waved.

"Hi, guys," he responded.

"Hey, so this is Sevie. I was telling you about her."

"Oh yes, our house guest - come in, come in! I've prepared a wonderful feast for us all."

Any nervousness I had felt went away as I stepped into his beautiful home. The open-plan kitchen opened up to a large, covered balcony and a yard with grass so perfect it looked fake. On the other side of the kitchen was a vast living room. We went upstairs to find two bedrooms, both decorated in all white, and a bathroom as big as the bedrooms with a round bathtub. "This is where you ladies will sleep," George said. "I'll sleep downstairs."

Melanie and I picked our rooms and washed up for dinner. George had cooked us pan-fried salmon with Mediterranean vegetables. We had a wonderful dinner that evening and talked into the late hours. Everything was fine until I woke up in the middle of the night with a panic attack. *Oh my gosh! I've got no money, no job, no home. It's only a matter of time before they find out, and they will kick me out onto the streets. I need to find a way to make money yesterday!* I dug my laptop out of my bag and frantically applied for a different position every minute. There was no way anyone living in

London would not know that Severine Desrosiers was job-hunting. The sleepless nights and panic attacks paid off; I received a call three days later from a call center company. They needed French speakers as soon as possible and paid weekly.

This will do for now. I'll hang out here for a while before going off to Australia, I thought.

But instead, I fell in love. I was in love with the city, the culture, and the many opportunities, and before I knew it, I had been in London for four years.

Although it had been even longer since we had physically seen each other, Diamond and I kept in contact. Even though we were on different continents, I kept her in the loop of everything I was doing. She knew all about my many job changes, relationships, and ups and downs in life, and I knew all about hers. We couldn't call each other more than once or twice a month, but when we did talk, it was for a minimum of three hours.

I had recently left a comfortable job as an office manager in a tech company for a better-paying one as a personal assistant in finance, thinking the grass was greener on the other side. I couldn't have been more wrong; the new job turned out to be horrible. It was an even smaller company than my former one, which I didn't like, with around fifty employees and every single one of them miserable. I had the type of egotistical psychopath of a boss you see in TV shows or movies. Every day was nothing short of a nightmare. I had to go to the bathroom several times a day to either hide from my boss, pray for Jesus to get me out, or cry.

Because she was the person I went to for advice, I told Diamond all about it, and she encouraged and motivated me to tough it out while looking for my escape route. Three weeks in, and one of the HR staff pulled me to the side to tell me it was not working, and it was my last day. It was as though his words removed the heavy shackles I had felt on my wrists and ankles since the first day I started there.

I felt lighter with every step I took away from that office. I wanted to call Diamond and tell her, but I knew that she would be starting her shift at that time, so I called another friend, Cindy, instead. Cindy and I met on a Nike group run one day. She was three years younger than me and had moved to London two years ago. We hit it off instantly; she was the first person I'd met in London who was of French Caribbean descent like me. "Hey Cindy! I was mentally ready to leave you a message – I'm surprised you can answer the phone at this time of day. You okay? I've got news!" I told her, excited despite what had just happened.

"Yeah, I'm all right. I've got news, too, but you first," she replied.

"So they've just let me go. I gotta tell you, I've never been happier – I'm finally free!" I yelled.

"Oh, wow! That's great; onto new adventures, I say."

"So what's your news?" I asked.

"Remember that waitressing job I was telling you about? Well, that's over."

I was unsure whether she was happy or disappointed; she'd told me several times how much she hated the job, but I knew about her strained financial situation.

"It's funny how much you and I have in common," she said, laughing. I chuckled right along with her at the thought of it all.

I went over to Cindy's house the next day to talk about different sites best suited for job searches. Our conversation quickly digressed to other topics, and because Diamond and Porsche happened to be on my mind, I started talking about them. I told Cindy how I'd met them, what their family was like, what happened to Porsche, and so on. Intrigued, Cindy sat and listened as I chatted on for a couple more hours before heading back home.

A few days later, I woke up to a message on Facebook from Porsche asking if I was available to talk. I was at Brody's, my ex-boyfriend's, house at the time, so I carefully climbed out of bed and tiptoed to the living room, leaving him asleep. *Oh I was just thinking about Porsche. I wonder if she is pregnant or something. That would be so cool,* I thought as I was dialing.

"Hey, Porsche – long-time no talk, what's up?"

"Sevie, are you alone?" she asked in a very serious voice.

"No, I'm actually at an ex-boyfriend's place."

"Okay, good; are you sitting down?"

"Yes, what's going on?" I asked as my curiosity grew by the second.

"Diamond got into a car accident last night. She's gone," she answered. I felt a punch in the gut, leaving me utterly breathless. Never in a million years had I expected such news. *Remember to breathe Sev, just breathe for now.* Realizing I had been holding my breath, I took a deep sigh and let out a cry, dropping the phone on the floor in the process. The tears blurred my eyesight. I heard Brody run into the room; he paused for a minute, then picked my phone up.

"Hello?" he said. "Um, she's not in a good state right now. She'll have to call you back." He hung up and took me in his arms without saying a word. The more I cried, the tighter he hugged me.

I calmed down enough to call Porsche back. Apparently Diamond was driving home from work and lost control of the vehicle which swerved into the opposite lane and hit another car head on. As Porsche was explaining this to me, I kept having to stop myself from asking her to pass the phone over to Diamond. We eventually hung up, as Porsche had to deliver the news to a couple more people. *Is this real? Am I in a nightmare?*

I stayed over at Brody's for a while, doing nothing but crying and sleeping. One day, a phone call interrupted my sobbing. I lifted my head from my pillow just enough to peek at who was calling. It was a recruiter. I sprang upright, wiped away my tears, and pushed my hair out of my face before answering the phone.

"Hello," I said, clearing my throat.

"Hi, Severine. It's Michelle from Tay Recruitment, how are you?"

"I'm fine," I answered, hoping that sounded believable.

"Severine, I've found a great role for you. It's a maternity cover, and this company is looking to hire as soon as possible. I'm going to send you the info. Please let me know if you are interested so we can possibly get you in to see them tomorrow. Is that okay?"

"Yes, that's fine, thanks," I replied. *That's great! I know I will ace this interview. Let me call Diamond and tell* – and just like an arrow piercing my heart, the pain came back all over again. I forced myself out of bed the next day and went through with the interview. I got hired on the spot, and they wanted me to start the next day.

As on most first days of work, I was a little nervous, but this time it was because I didn't know if I would break down in tears. I did not want to be the new girl whose best friend had died, so I decided not to mention this to anyone. When I walked into the office, I saw my team waiting for me with smiles on their faces. Madeline, one of the receptionists, was tasked with my induction. She walked me around the office, stopping to meet a few key people before showing me to my desk.

"I'll make us some tea, and when I get back, I'll show you

how to log in," she said with a large smile.

I sat on the black leather chair and stared into the nothingness. *What happens now?* I asked myself. Diamond kept me level-headed; she was one of the few people who were just as weird as I was. When I felt down, she lifted me up. Losing her was like getting punched in the stomach with no chance of ever catching your breath again. We had made plans, Diamond and I, set ourselves goals we had yet to achieve. Still, I was ever so thankful to have had the privilege of knowing her for thirteen amazing years. Her untimely death helped me understand how Diamond life is. Life is Diamond. *From now on, I have to live in the moment and be thankful for the happy times, because I don't know how long they will last. I've come a very long way from thinking I would be the girl that would live in the same town her whole life. Losing her is painful but like everything else in life I will get through this. With everything I've been through already I know I can handle whatever else life throws at me so bring it on!*

"Severine? You there?" The receptionist asked as she waved her hand in my face to get my attention.

"Huh?"

"You zoned out there for a minute. You ready for me to show you how to log in?"

"Yes, I'm ready."

MEET THE AUTHOR

Severine's initial idea of becoming an author first came into play after a conversation in the kitchen with her mom. Her mother felt she had a story to tell which would make a good book, but neither of them had any idea life would have evolved the way it did. After years of hesitancy, Severine eventually put pen to paper, and a memoir was born.

A finance employee/University student by day and writer by night, this first-time author likes to dabble in fashion, work on starting a business, and spend time with friends and family in her spare time.

Find out more about Severine at:

 www.severinedesrosiers.com
 @sevie1986
 Severine Desrosiers

Printed in Great Britain
by Amazon